The Fishmonger's Daughter

Tim Collie

ISBN 978-0-578-03996-1 (pbk.)
1. Biography

First Paperback Edition

Table of Contents

Preface — My 80th Birthday . . . 5
Chapter 1 — Katsuko . . . 7
Chapter 2 — My Father . . . 12
Chapter 3 — The Fish . . . 15
Chapter 4 — Just A Girl . . . 19
Chapter 5 — The New Boy . . . 23
Chapter 6 — Bonkura . . . 27
Chapter 7 — The War . . . 30
Chapter 8 — A Battle . . . 35
Chapter 9 — The Bomb . . . 41
Chapter 10 — A Brighter Future . . . 45
Chapter 11 — First Love . . . 49
Chapter 12 — Elopement . . . 54
Chapter 13 — Life Away From Home . . . 59
Chapter 14 — With Child . . . 63
Chapter 15 — Hard Times . . . 66
Chapter 16 — Back To Yatsushiro . . . 71
Chapter 17 — New Life In Sales . . . 76
Chapter 18 — Design School . . . 80
Chapter 19 — Bar Girl . . . 84
Chapter 20 — My First Property . . . 87
Chapter 21 — My American Husband . . . 91
Chapter 22 — The Big Apple . . . 96
Chapter 23 — Kazunori . . . 100
Chapter 24 — Suzu Fashion . . . 105
Chapter 25 — The Corcoran Group . . . 108
Chapter 26 — Sales Strategy . . . 115
Chapter 27 — Clients And Friends . . . 129
Chapter 28 — Getting My Broker's License . . . 134
Chapter 29 — Today . . . 139

In Loving Memory of My Father the Fishmonger
and my Mother, Wife Number One

PREFACE

My 80th Birthday

As I looked around the room, all I could see were familiar, loving faces shrouded by illness, infirmity, and approaching death. It was natural, I suppose; we were all getting up in age. I was approaching my 80th birthday, and here I was back in my hometown for the *sanjusankaiki* - the ceremony that marks the 33rd year after my mother's death.

The conversation dwelled on death, not life; illness, not health. It was all really too much.

"Now, you lot, listen here," I said, raising my voice so even the deaf could hear. "I'm going to continue working in real estate until I'm one hundred years old. And then, when I am one hundred, I'm going to become a movie actress. What am I going to do if you're not there to watch my movie debut with me, eh?"

My friends sighed and smiled.

"Ahh, Kacchan, you have your health, you'll be okay," one said.

"Well then, we'll have to all make sure we live that long, eh?" said another. "Come on everybody let's stay strong and healthy until Kacchan makes it as a movie star."

And so this reunion that started off as cheery as a wake, really started going.

"We can't die until Kacchan becomes an actress," another of my friends added. Then and there, they all pledged to go on living.

At one point, I said much of the same thing to my mentor Barbara Corcoran, the former president of the Corcoran Group.

"When I'm a hundred years old I'm going to become an actress," adding, "I'm not sure if it will be a love story, though."

Barbara just smiled back and said, "You can do it, Katsuko! Never give up the fight." By then, she had grown accustomed to my admittedly eccentric notions about life, love, and New York real estate. She had been patient with me during a long dry spell when I first got into the business. She had deferred to my ideas about selling to Japanese clients before I had proved myself. She had trusted me and gave me the time, courage, inspiration, and freedom to succeed or fail on my own at her company. I owe her a lot for that.

What I told my friends back in Yatsushiro — that wasn't B.S. My current goal is to continue working in the real estate business until I'm one hundred years old. Then I will make my screen debut as an actress. New York, of course, is the center of the theater world. But I want my old friends to see me, and I figure that few will be able to make it to New York when they hit the century mark.

Foolish, you say? I figure Hollywood will be a breeze. How is it that, as I pass my eightieth birthday, I can still make it in the cutthroat world of the New York real estate business? How is it that a fishmonger's daughter from Kumamoto in southern Japan came, through thick and thin, to live in New York in the first place?

I have traveled so far in my life, and I have learned so much along the way. This is what I want to share with you.

CHAPTER 1

Katsuko

My parents wished they had never given birth to a girl, because I was nothing but trouble growing up. In Japan at that time, a girl was a burden, not a blessing, and I was perhaps the biggest burden of them all. So they raised me like just another son. My father dressed me like a boy, worked me like an apprentice, and taught me to run his fish business like his eldest son. His other sons were never interested.

My hair was cut like a boy's. I wore no ribbons, and my scruffy backpack wasn't pink like all the other girls who lived on our narrow street. I was dressed in black pants just like my three brothers and sent off on errands hours before any other child my age ever stirred. I was six years old.

The most important of these errands was searching for my father. My routine every morning was to wake up and look for wherever he had slept the night before: with one of his other wives, a new girlfriend perhaps, a geisha house or even the local jail. He was a big man in our tiny village, the owner of the largest fish market, the head of the black market, a great cook and a wonderful character. Being so popular made him hard to find at times for my mother, and she sent me out nearly every morning after sunrise to find him. Boats would be arriving with fish, our telephone would be ringing with orders, and he was sorely needed.

When I look back on my life, and try to figure out what pushed me from this tiny fishing village, to postwar Tokyo and eventually New York, I always come back to my father, and those early morning journeys to find him.

The bicycle I used was old and I hated riding over the rocky roads and wooden bridges that ringed and ran across the canals of our village, Yatsushiro. It was so very hard to peddle this rusty bike over the gravel that lined the canals in Yatsushiro. I got tired very quickly because it was just so difficult for my tiny legs to turn the wheels of the old bike. Growing up, I always thought I lived in a large city because Yatsushiro seemed so big to a little girl, and I had to ride all around it looking for my father.

I didn't really know much about life at first, and nothing about marriage, of course, but at that time a man could still have more than one wife in Japan. There had been laws passed to make this illegal, but the reality was that it was quite common in rural areas. It was a sign of prominence, especially among businessmen. If you wanted everyone to know that you were successful, if you were making a lot of money, you wanted to show that you could support more than one woman. These wives didn't live together—that never happened in Japan—which made it all the more expensive. You had to buy them all houses. Also, remember that Japan was very poor back then, and there were so many children, and probably more girls than boys. Again, a girl wasn't anything but a burden. There was no work that a single woman could do to live, and it was probably better for everyone if men could support more than one. For poor families, too, it was more honorable than selling your daughter to the geisha houses.

But my father was pretty smart, always thinking about the bottom line. He turned his wives into businesses, setting them up with fish stands all around the countryside. He franchised them, just like McDonald's. That way they could bring in some money. He was always thinking like that. I remember, when I was older, hearing people talking about my father and saying what a good businessman he was because he supported so many women, and had them working in his business, too.

My mother was his "Number One" wife. There were four in all at that time, so I was always pedaling off to see Numbers Two, Three and sometimes Four. I didn't understand what was going on at first. All I knew then is that I hated getting up hours before any of the other girls in town.

I remember the very first time, my mother waking me up and telling me I have to go search for father. This house she sent me to, it took me about thirty minutes riding just to get there. I went up, banged on the door and this strange, drowsy woman opened it. Her name was Toshi Oba-san, or Aunt Toshi. It's common in Japan to call all women of a certain age 'aunt' regardless of whether there is any blood relation or not.

She was my father's Number Three wife. She was a very ugly woman to me, with a large head and a fat, thick face and jowls that shook like a walrus when she lumbered back and forth. At other times, when she was angry, she became a blowfish, puffing up those cheeks to twice the size of her head. I thought of my father as handsome. I still do. I don't know what he saw in such an ugly woman. Later, when my mother and Toshi Oba-san came to blows in the street, I would wonder if he really thought it was worth the bother to be involved with so many women. It seemed like very hard work, far from any pleasure it may have given him.

I guess I woke them up. Looking past Toshi Oba-san, I could see my dad rolling over on the floor behind her. I said to my father, "You have to come home because there is a telephone call from your business partner." He was still groggy and wasn't in a good mood. Maybe he was angry because my mother had sent me here, because this was Number Three wife, after all. "I'm coming," he'd say. "Go back to your mother." Then the woman smiled and gave me one *sen*, which was like giving a kid a quarter back then. Or by the formula I knew best: one sen = three pieces of candy. I was amazed at the sight of my father — and even more amazed at the easy money — but I instinctively knew I better not mention this to my mother. I didn't fully understand why my father was sleeping at somebody else's house.

This became my routine. Sometimes I'd go to the fourth wife's house and father wouldn't be there. She was usually very nice, but at these times you could tell she was a little perturbed, a little sad. After all, if he wasn't at first wife's home, and he wasn't with second wife, where was he? (I'm still not sure how many of these wives knew each other.) Sometimes she'd get mad at me and I knew I wasn't going to get my quarter. So I'd go back to my mother. She'd sigh, look down at her feet, and say something like, "Get on over to Matsudaka village then." So off I'd go to another woman's house, this time far on the other side of town. This was another hour of bicycle riding, and sometimes I hadn't even had breakfast. Again another strange woman would open the door and finally I'd see my dad sleeping inside. By this time, I recall, I was really confused that my father seemed to be sleeping at so many different houses. Maybe this was just something all fathers did—left their house sometime after supper to sleep somewhere else. But eventually I knew it was wrong, and I do recall the sadness, not wanting to tell anybody about my father and his strange habit. I'd probably noticed that my friends' fathers seemed to be waking up in the same house with them in the morning.

Strangely, it was only me who did this. My brothers were never asked to go. But my mom always knew where the women were. She always had the right house, the right street. I was never lost, but I did get tired of this. On some days I would make three or four sen — an unusual day, to be sure, when my father had perhaps discovered a new conquest that the other mistresses were unaware of — but I wanted to sleep in like my brothers and the other kids. Getting up so early to chase wives and geishas was exhausting. I was still tired when I got to school, and my studies suffered. "Why am I doing this," I'd whine to my mom. "Why don't you ask one of them?" I'd say, pointing to my sleeping brothers. But she'd only tell me not to talk back, so all I had to look forward to was hoping each time that my father was at Toshi Oba-san's house so I'd get my one sen. I realize I saw so much that I never understood until now.

CHAPTER 2

My Father

My father was a very strong, popular, powerful man in the life of our village — a small-town Lothario, too. Easy-going to the outside world, yes. But he had a very bad temper with my mother, my brothers and I. Our family life was not an ideal one, though I was proud of my father's place in the village, and his skills with fish. But living in a house with such a man came with a price.

My mother was a very sad, very unhappy woman. She was saddled with us children, an uncaring, adulterous man, and his ingrate parents. That may have been the life of most women in Japan at that time. I just don't know. Once, I visited one of my favorite aunts and even discovered my father there. He seemed to be sleeping with every woman in the prefecture.

By 1933, the year I started peddling about, searching for my father, Japan's imperial army was rampaging through China and Southeast Asia. The war was popular, but it took a toll at home. Food was scarce for many, even for us in the fish shop at times, and Japan was very much still an overpopulated, underdeveloped country with many mouths to feed. That was where my father came in. He was a denizen of the "water trade", the shadowy culture of bars, brothels and geisha houses that, in truth, really held everything together. As the leading fish wholesaler in the area, he was the chief supplier of fish for the regional mafia, the Yakuza. Physically, he wasn't a big man, but he had these thick eyebrows that you saw coming long before he was in front of you. He had the butch cut of a Yakuza, a gangster. He wasn't Yakuza himself, but he walked with the exaggerated swagger—back straight, chest out, legs wide apart and toes pointing outward—that telegraphed power back in those days. Geisha's would always walk by our shop in the late afternoon, on their way to work no doubt, chirping, "Is-san, Is-san, Hello Is-san", in sexy, singsong voices that suggested many a night spent laughing over fine sake and eel. Geisha girls were always singling him out when we were walking in the crowded streets—Is-san! Is-san! Is-san! The geishas, of course, were so mysterious and forbidden to a little girl then, and I remember wondering how did all these geishas know my father. After all, they never bought fish at our shop.

But those were the circles in which my father traveled. Boss Horikawa, who I called uncle, was a powerful Yakuza and a frequent, very loud guest at our home. And on those occasions when my father might be arrested for smuggling or some other black market activity, a policeman would show up at our door with a list of food and drink for the inevitable party he'd be throwing at the jail. Whatever was thrown at him, my father just rolled with the punches. When I was eight, one of his business deals went bad and we lost our house — a wonderful manse in one of the best parts of town. Because of my father's role in the business, he was often called on to guarantee loans for other merchants. When one of these loans went bad, and the merchant he had guaranteed fled to Taiwan, we had to give up that house. Losing it was one of my earliest painful memories, and perhaps my first introduction to the risks inherent in running any business. In the garden behind the house was a pomelo tree — a plant native to Asian countries that grows the largest citrus fruit in the world. When it was in fruit, the tree would be heavily laden with pomelos — big, green, lantern shaped fruit — the size of a child's head. For years after we left that house, I'd pester my parents by saying to them - in my broad Yatsushiro dialect - *Nande kotoshiwa zabon torini ikarento?* — "Why can't we go and pick the pomelos this year?"

We had lost our house. And yet my father didn't have the slightest care in the world, acting as if nothing had happened.

CHAPTER 3

The Fish

We moved to a rented two-story house in the Kangyuji Temple area of Shioya that actually became the rear of our new fish market. It, too, was a big house for those days, located in the front of a Buddhist temple where the neighborhood children played. You walked through the fish shop, past the tables crammed with tuna, with eel and octopus, around a huge refrigerator and through piles of empty, smelly boxes before you entered our home. To your left was a small room where we kept our telephone and where my father counted money late at night. The bottom floor was essentially a single central room where we slept – my parents, my brothers and me. My grandparents slept upstairs along with my mother's spinster aunt. At the rear of the house was a tiny kitchen, and just outside was a big well with a heavy metal pump attached. I remember the pump very well because I had to use it so often. A fish shop needs a lot of water, so it seemed I was always running back to pump more water. It was tough on my skinny arms—they were always so sore—but as I said, my parents raised me as something like a boy, but less than a son.

And then dad started a catering business. I was only six years old, but he started training me as a chef. He seemed to look around at all his sons, then at me, and decided that I was the type of person who would take over the fish business. It wasn't a hard choice. My brothers were quite adamant that they'd never be caught dead cutting a piece of fish for a living. It was beneath them and, like most rural children, they were bored with the lives of their parents. We all wanted to set out for the big city. My brothers were always fighting any chores involving the smell of fish, the cleaning of fish, the preparing of fish—anything but the eating of fish.

But I was always in the fish store, and since I was the one constantly fetching my dad away from his liaisons, sooner or later it stood to reason he might look upon me as a willing apprentice. I was usually just sitting there anyway, watching his dealings with customers but especially the way he could take an ordinary fish and turn it into a work of art—a flower, a sculpture, even a building. He could not only make the fish come back to life, but actually give it the ability to converse, it seemed, with the person who was about to consume it.

One day, when I was about six years old, he saw me playing around with the sashimi knife and called me over. He grabbed another knife, picked up a fish, and started filleting it very slowly, explaining why he was doing this and that. He then positioned the knife correctly in my tiny hands and together we cut up a sardine. It was like music, with its own tempo and rhythm. I was silent, expressionless, like so many Japanese children in the presence of their stern elders. But inside was I giddy. My dad was a very serious man when it came to fish. This was the imparting of an ancient, secret knowledge, and I had to be very careful. If he thought I wasn't paying attention, or taking this task seriously, he'd end it right there.

I think he could see some glistening of talent inside me. Or at least I like to imagine he did, writing this six decades later. I want to believe he thought I was good at this—not just interested, not just a lonely girl basking in a parent's rare glow. I'll never know.

But it was fascinating to me, this fish business. I was so intrigued learning that, when a customer came to buy fish, there was always a right and wrong way to put it up on the scale. I played for days with the scale, mimicking my father's actions exactly, and practiced weighing all the different kinds of fish we sold in the store.

There was no detail too small for me to master. I learned the techniques particular to each creature: *Tai. Saba. Aji. Maguro. Buri. Ebi. Iwashi. Tako. Hamachi.* To me, it was like playing house—what all the other girls my age were doing—only my house was real. My kitchen was real, and all the other adults came to play with me in it.

Dad would spend the longest time observing my technique, but it was quite a while before we got off of sardines. They're simple, because, really, they don't involve much skill. But father made it clear that a mastery of sardine technique was essential to moving upward in the fish trade. First, you'd break off the tiny head, but you had to do it just right, with a swift, strong movement. Then you'd remove the intestines and stripped the meat off the tiny bones.

When I was about ten, I started cutting for customers. I still couldn't do big fish. The apprentices would handle that. Each fish demanded its own way to be cut. Red snapper required a lot of work. It was the biggest fish I was allowed to work on. But for my tiny fingers, it required a lot of patience. The trick was always making sure the meat didn't come off with the bones.

I worked after school. My father was very strict, but he taught me well. He used to hit me—that was common back then—and he never praised me. I remember cutting myself a lot. I was bleeding and crying and he never said anything. But I kept working very hard.

Designs were something that I dreamed of making at that time. I used to sit in marvel watching my father, trying to duplicate his skill. He used to make a nice design with the Tai using bamboo. It would make it seem like the fish was jumping off the plate. On other plates, he made it look like the creature was flying off the water.

He would also put the fish in ice cold water, then boiling hot water, and cut it in such a way that it looked as if it were unfurling like the petals of a flower. You put the red ginger in the middle of the flower and make it look like a rose.

One of his most famous creations was the depiction of the *Meoto-iwa*, or the "wedded rocks" in a seaside town called *Futamigaura.* This famous landmark—two rocks that represent male and female—symbolize the mythical first married couple in Japanese history in the Shinto religion. The sun rises between these two rocks, and many Japanese like to go to the beach at sunup to see this famous site. The rocks are joined together by sacred ropes called *shimenawa,* which are made from braided rice stalks. It is a site that every Japanese is familiar with and my father's depiction of these rocks on the seafood plate was well-known throughout our small town. He became very famous for this design, and even though it was costly and time-consuming, many of his important customers requested it for weddings and other important gatherings.

He was an artist doing this, a Picasso with fish. He was very serious and very temperamental and if I asked too many questions he'd get mad. But I was so intrigued by everything he did. I wanted to get all the answers at that very moment.

He never praised me. I remember crying cutting the fish. I was bleeding but he never said anything. I did not want to quit. I don't like to fail. So I kept working hard.

CHAPTER 4

Just A Girl

By the standards of the time, we were middle class. There were only three or four phones in the entire region at this time, and we had one. Our phone number was 323 and my father always seemed to be talking on it, usually early in the morning or in the evening just after the close of business.

He didn't actually talk but yelled, the lines were so poor, and that became a running joke in the neighborhood. Often when he was talking he'd yell, "And this is a big secret, so don't tell anyone! Absolutely no one. Don't tell anyone!" He actually thought he was whispering, but this could be heard all over the street! The neighbors would come up and joke, "Don't tell anyone! It's a big secret." What was he always talking about? I assume business or some scheme he had cooked up, since it was clear there were no secrets needed when it came to women.

My mom was always so busy. She was handling everything herself, running the house, running the business. I suppose many Japanese women her age went through this, but it was through my mother's eyes that I saw how hard the life of a woman was. My mother was tall and thin, and I always thought she was very pretty. But she always looked tired and sad. I don't really ever remember her laughing by herself or even with somebody. She was always handling everything in the house, which wasn't easy because she had to take care of my grandparents, and especially *Mine* (mee-nay) *Oba-san*, my grandfather's sister, my great aunt. Aunt Mine was very mean, and was always complaining about something. Mine Oba-san never married and she was quite the spinster. She'd complain that the rice was hard, or that the miso soup was too thin. She'd just walk around the neighborhood all day and complain about everything. But my mom had no say. She couldn't talk back. That was simply the way it was then.

Though we weren't poor, and we did live in a nice part of the village, it became very clear to me at an early age that there was an important difference between the daughter of a dressmaker, the daughter of a shoemaker, and me—the daughter of a fishmonger. Across the street from our home was a very nice dress shop, and a kimono shop. Down the street were several cobblers who made beautiful shoes. I used to stand and stare every morning at their pretty daughters, holding their mothers' hands as they walked to school. They had nice pleated skirts, and pink and white sweaters. They usually wore a pink bow in their hair, and they had pink socks with their shiny shoes. They were so beautiful!

I was always wearing pants. Black pants. Black pants that had belonged to my brothers. And a black backpack, or a *randoseru.* This was the most important item a child could have, but it became the symbol of my shame. In Japan, the child's backpack is an important gift, a rite of passage even, that he or she carries off on their first day of school and independence. Parents who want the best for their children, pick the best randoserus, and spend a small fortune. It's as important as your uniform and your shoes. At this time, girls always had red or pink randoserus. And boys had black. It was just so common, but I alone had to lug this old black backpack that my brothers had tossed aside. If anything said to the world what my parents thought of me, this was it.

I wanted a pink backpack! I couldn't say so and, I couldn't really protest, because my mom would just yell at me. So I went to school crying everyday. It would only get worse once I got to class, because all the kids would start teasing me. Here I was this tired dirty little girl, dressed all in black, like a boy, with a boy's backpack and none of the pretty little things a girl usually has. I don't think I ever had a ribbon tied in my hair, which is extraordinary for a little girl, especially a little girl in Japan. It seemed to me that every mother was putting ribbons in their daughters' hair. That wherever I looked, all I saw was pretty little girls with white dresses and pinks ribbons. On top of everything else I often got teased because I had thick, wavy hair—they called it "American hair" back then, and that wasn't meant as a compliment. Everyone hated the Americans. A Japanese girl was supposed to have straight, fine hair. So everyone hated my hair.

We weren't poor, but my family just didn't care about girls. Americans never understand this. Girls just weren't that important. We were a burden, not a blessing. But to me having a dress, a pink backpack—these were the most important things in the world. For six months this went on, until I was crying so much I didn't ever want to go to school again. I was being teased everyday. But my mom and dad just didn't care. They said it was a waste of money. The only time I ever got to wear a dress, anything approaching a girl's clothes, was during festival time. But even then they were old, used kimonos.

I have this very vivid memory of putting one on for the first time. I was so excited. Here I was finally dressing like a girl! I lay the package on the floor and unwrap the kimono very carefully, taking care not to get it dirty. I sit there and look at it for a while. I'm breathing hard, for it seems like everything is going to change now. I'm going to be a girl! So I put it on so very very slowly. I pull on it a little. It seems too tight. And short. Way too short. My legs are showing! And then I begin to notice the wear, the small, frayed spots, and the stains. My parents hadn't even bothered to buy me a new kimono, or even find me one that was the right size. I was so embarrassed having to walk around the festival with a kimono so short you could see my ankles.

I had three brothers, but in all, there were six boys with me in the house most of the time. That's because my father had two young apprentices, or *de-chi,* who lived in the small room in the attic at the front of the house. This was quite common, because there were so many poor children. So, parents would loan their children out to work. You called the practice *kuchi-harashi*, literally "cutting out mouths" to feed in a family.

My three brothers were Kazuo, Hideo, and Hiroshi. We generally got along, but again, I was caught between two worlds. I was not quite a girl since I dressed like a boy, but I wasn't a boy and I was never going to grow up in their world of privileges. My brothers got far more time to study than I ever did, and that merely nursed my anger. They were being groomed to go further and farther than my father, and if that failed, they'd inherit the fish business. But as I said, none of them were really interested in fish like I was, so it was a double blow to me knowing that I'd never grow to be someone of my father's stature—that was made clear to all girls early on. On top of that, I had the apprentices to contend with, and then later, yet another boy entered our troubled household.

CHAPTER 5

The New Boy

When I was seven or eight years old, my father came home one day with a young boy who I first thought was just another apprentice, even though he looked younger than me. It was in the middle of the afternoon and my father called everyone into the house. "This boy is coming to live with us. His name is Hideichi, my father said sternly, as if he were addressing employees. "From now on, he is a member of our family, and we're going to treat him like family."

I could tell everyone was in shock. My mother was quietly sobbing. My grandparents and Mine Oba-san were all looking very uncomfortable. They were staring at their feet. Their reactions were all very proper, very traditionally Japanese, but you could feel the shame and tension in the air.

Hideichi was my father's son with his "Number Two" wife, a woman whom I had not visited too much recently, but whom I knew about. The story, I learned later, was that she had found a new husband who didn't want her child. She could only get married if she got rid of the boy. My father didn't really have a choice, and he probably looked upon Hideichi as one more worker and much cheaper than an apprentice or the cost of supporting his second wife. In his ledger, he turned a liability into an asset.

My brothers had been aware of Hideichi for some time before he came to live with us. In fact, they seemed aware—along with the rest of the town — of the illicit spawn my father had left with mistresses throughout the region. I still remember, years later, one of my brothers speaking of the shame he felt attending the same kindergarten with one of these half brothers. My mother was not the sort of woman to voice an open, clear objection to looking after the child of a mistress; she would make her anger and humiliation felt in other ways. But whether my father understood my mother's feelings in this matter, he was, as always, easygoing about the entire business. I doubt that he lost sleep over how he could make this situation less of a burden for my mother. After all, he was the man of the house and my mother's inconveniences were her own and of little consequence to his life.

I never thought of him as a brother, just another one of the *de-chi*. It was clear that my mother thought even less of him. She was obviously angry and jealous. Imagine, having to raise one of the children of your husband's concubines! Her hatred became clearer to me as time went on. I started to notice how she isolated and humiliated Hideichi more and more.

Every morning before school, my mom would pack our lunch boxes, the traditional *obentos* that all Japanese children carried off to school. The meal was always two pieces of fish and rice. One day, though, my brother Hiroshi opened his lunch box and found only one piece of fish inside. I asked my mother about this. "Oh, that's Hideichi's" she said. She'd been giving him less food than her other children. She made me swear never to tell my father. Another time I was told to prepare the *obentos* for everyone, and my mother ordered me to make sure Hideichi only got one piece of fish. At first, I don't think the hatred of this act really dawned on me. I'm not sure I would have understood such hatred at this age. But more and more I could see how she treated my younger stepbrother. Every day when we got home from school my mother would give us all a piece of candy, but Hideichi would get nothing; one time I actually remember her telling us to eat it fast before he got home so he wouldn't see it. "Hurry up and put these in your mouths!' she'd yell. She'd make a show of it—her hatred was that great. My mother didn't even treat the apprentices this poorly. That's when I realized Hideichi was someone apart from us; he would never be family.

The abuse had its intended effect. Hideichi was a terrible student, worse than even me. My mother was always telling him to do this and that while the other boys studied so he didn't really have time to study, and quite frankly, I'm not sure he would have anyway. He was very sad and very angry, and he often lashed out. He'd get into fights and steal items that didn't belong to him. I remember for the longest time he didn't really know who his mother was, as my mother made it very clear to him it wasn't her. He had been left behind, and like some lost child in a fairy tale, he wanted to believe there was a mother out there looking for him. He'd run around the streets going up to random women asking if they were his mom, or if they knew where his mother was. Only very rarely did his real mother show up to give him something. She'd be very stealth like about her occasional encounters with her son, which surreptitiously took place just around the corner from our house. I guess she didn't want my mother, or maybe my father, to see her. But Hideichi never seemed to see her long enough to remember her face and I don't think she ever told him that she was his mother. She just appeared out of the market crowd, gave him a piece of candy, tugged his cheek and melted away. He'd continue to paw at other women who passed by.

There was no running water back then, and as I said before, a fish business needs so much water. He was always pumping water, at least when I wasn't. All of this – the hard work, my mother's cruelty, his yearning for his own mother – took a toll on the boy. He grew more and more angry, got into fights, and would do nasty things to me and the others such as steal our things, rip our clothes, and hit us when we weren't looking.

CHAPTER 6

Bonkura

In Yatsushiro, the dumber you were, the more your parents made you study. This was especially true for girls; parents thought that the stupid girls would never get married and become a burden they'd have to carry to old age. It did happen from time to time; just look at how my father ended up having to feed Mine Oba-san. Everyone in the family was ashamed once it became known that a daughter was studying harder because it announced to everyone with a son that she was stupid and not good marriage material.

I was not a good student, and my parents never failed to tell me how stupid I was. *Bonkura*—"stupid" in the regional dialect—was all I ever heard growing up. *Bonkura bonkura bonkura*—my parents just thought I was such an idiot. I'd overhear my mother chatting with the neighbors, and she'd laugh, shake her head, and tell them how smart her boys were but how stupid her daughter was. Soon it became quite common knowledge that Takenaga's daughter was an idiot. The neighbors, who didn't want their sons thinking of marrying me, told me I was dumb and all of their children chimed in as well. I began to truly believe I was dumb.

To me it was pretty clear why I wasn't doing well in school; I had to get up early every morning to look for my dad. I really resented having to wake up so early, and I was always tired so I never felt like studying. When I finally found him, we always came back and started preparing the morning's fish before I finally went to school. To be honest, I didn't like books at that time, and I probably wouldn't have sat around reading but I was never given the chance. Childhood should be about discovery, but there was no time for me to discover books. My day was already full. Also, I resented how well my brothers did in school and that they had time to study. I rebelled and didn't even try to compete with them.

When I was twelve, it was time to take the exams necessary to enter the best schools. It was 1940, and by then it was clear we were going to war with America. Everything on the radio, in the classroom, and in the posters all over town advertised that America was the enemy. It was also pretty clear that I was not going to do well on my exams, but my parents paid to send me to a nightly preparatory class (commonly called cram school) anyway.

The cram school known as a *juku* in Japanese was held at the house of a girl whose mother was the top servant to one of the area's best families. It was taught by a teacher at my school and specifically held for the "stupid" girls whose marriage prospects might be hurt if they didn't score well on the exams.

Like so many other episodes of my life, the lessons being taught were not the lessons I chose to learn. We covered all the topics—grammar, history, math—but what I remember most was the breaks we took after one hour. It was then that the top servant would serve these delicious Western or American cakes to us. Oh, how I loved these cakes. I think it was right then and there that I got my first taste of the West. I was bored during the classes, but I would ask so many questions about these cakes. The servant had studied in Tokyo, and that's where she learned to make these cakes.

I asked so many questions that I think everyone around me who had been watching this *bonkura* girl was surprised that I'd finally come to life. All I looked forward to during this time was going to the *juku* and having one of these cakes.

And then I failed the exam.

Twice.

So now it was confirmed: the daughter of Takenaga was indeed an idiot; don't marry her. I took this hard but stupidity became my universe; I accepted it. There was nothing I could do, so I applied and was accepted to a local business school. That exam was easy—it was the school for all the castoffs anyway. But it also was the right choice for me because I loved business. My father had raised me with an eye on running his business. He had taught me everything about the fish market from the time I could walk, and I was very intrigued by this idea of taking a dollar and turning into two. However, this wasn't supposed to be a woman's role at the time, and even at thirteen I knew I was being crossed off the list as a marriage prospect by most of the neighborhood.

That's why it came as a big shock to my parents when I started to do well in my classes. Soon I was one of the top students at the school. It was a fairly useful class unlike history or literature. I could put into practice what I was learning everyday at the fish market. I learned to properly calculate profit, reduce costs, and find the right price; all the things you need to know in running a business. A lot of this was second nature to my father. I don't think he ever had the luxury of a classroom. Auspiciously I came into my own at the school. I could see now that I did have some brains, and that life just might have a path for me after all.

But did this ever get around to the neighbors? No. Once you're labeled, especially in a small country town, you pretty much stay labeled. That's the way of a village and the big reason rural life is so stifling. If you're on top, like my father, nothing could be better. But I was an accumulator of experiences. I held grudges, remembered slights, and knew that someday soon I would have to leave Yatsushiro.

CHAPTER 7

The War

I came of age during the rise and fall and rise again of Japan. My childhood was spent in schools awash in the propaganda of a militaristic state, one that had conquered China and was sweeping over the rest of Southeast Asia. My teenage years were spent paying the price, with so many others, for our leader's evil. In addition to learning the glories of empire, we were also trained to kill, to stab, beat, and disembowel enemy soldiers who might land by parachute outside our school yard. And my years as a young woman—again, like so many others—were spent in both the domestic and political turmoil of the American occupation of my country. I've seen the best and worst that both countries have to offer, and I believe, my life has been spent on a high wire stretched between them. If at times I've lost my balance, I've never lost my grip. I've never fallen off and when the rope has swayed beneath me, I've merely climbed back on it again.

The backdrop to this girlhood was the imperial expansion of the Japanese throughout Asia. The country had already conquered and colonized Korea and Korean slave laborers—used as farm hands, factory laborers and office workers—were a part of everyday life even in Yatsushiro. The conquest of Manchuria, or northeastern China, in 1931 colored much of my childhood, as it provided the basis for much of what we learned in school. The truth was that my country was desperate for raw materials like oil, iron, and coal to keep our economic footing, but this plunder of other nations' wealth was depicted to boys and girls as the country's glorious mission to civilize all of Asia under the banner of the Rising Sun.

Our curriculums were laden with this drivel, and our playtimes were spent rehearsing air raid drills and survival skills—killing with bayonets—for the larger war that everyone knew was coming. The daily curriculum included training in the use of native weapons like the *katana*, the *nunchaku*, the *bo*, and the *kendo*. Japan had claimed that its taking of Manchuria was a liberation, and it set up a socialistic utopia called Manchukuo that I heard much about as a child. Events like the Rape of Nanking, which occurred when I was twelve in 1938, were restaged for us as exciting battles to save the Chinese from themselves. It would take me years to purge all of this out of my system. What I remember most from these years is the sense of superiority we all had, even in my tiny village.

I've never thought much about the war and the paths that it opened for me. You don't want to look at something so dire and deadly for the opportunities it might have granted you. But I can't imagine what my life would have been like if there had been no war, or if Japan had won. This horrible conflict came just as I was entering adulthood, and it seemed to set up a course for me that would carry me far out of this village and eventually, out of my culture and country.

Your country is the only thing you know, as a child, and it's really difficult to remember exactly what you realized when. What I do realize looking back is how isolated, how brainwashed we all were growing up in such a system. Life was a series of slogans, printed in newspapers, pasted on the walls of classrooms and shouted out from the nearest radio. Japan was God's Country—you heard it over and over and over. All that was foreign, all that was western—was materialistic, corrupt, and ultimately, evil. We were embarking on a noble endeavor in our conquests of Korea, of China and the rest of Asia, and it was the Americans who sought to deter us from our glorious course. Slogans. Slogans. Slogans. "Luxury is the Enemy" was one you heard a lot, because it was clear that we weren't living in luxury as this war progressed.

We also had many different rituals—rooted in Buddhism, and Shinto, the native Japanese religion—to survive this war. One I remember most was the "100 Steps", a prayer for luck we frequently used for my uncle, who was fighting the war in China. You'd pick up a small stone at the *Tori,* the entrance to the shrine, and take it through the gate. You'd do this one hundred times, back and forth through the gate. It was a fun game for a child.

Another ritual was known as *Sen-nin Bari*, or the 1,000-person stitches. When a young man was called off to duty, the women in his family would make two things for him to take along for good luck. The first was a flag signed by his family, friends, and co-workers. The second was the sen-nin bari, a charm belt. You'd take a red thread and a blue cloth and then ask as many people as possible to make a single stitch. You had to do this 1,000 times—find 1,000 people to ask—as a prayer for luck for a loved one in the war. But, if you found someone who was born in the Year of the Dragon, that person could make as many stitches as his age. So, a forty-year-old could give you forty stitches! And if you found a woman born in the year of the Tiger, she could sew in twelve stitches. That's why they were sometimes called Tiger belts. The task itself was the prayer, the product, the material symbol of the luck you had created for your son or daughter in the war. If worn, we believed the belt would protect our brothers from death, and give them courage. They wore these belts beneath their uniforms. This was very popular. Every family was doing it.

You can't imagine the propaganda, the fervor, and the fear. I was just a young girl becoming a woman, and certainly no bookworm in this backwater town, but even I started to realize what a strange, corrupting air we lived in. At the business school, we began to wear military uniforms. Boys wore soldier's uniforms while we girls wore kimonos that had been cut to form pants, call monpai. In addition to studies, we began to get training in self-defense, basically how to kill the soldiers who might invade our village. The boys got more intense drilling, but girls were given bamboo shoots sharpened into spears and taught how to deal a deathblow quickly and efficiently to an American. After that, we were told that we had to kill ourselves. Don't Show Your Shame, our drill instructors told us over and over again. Don't allow yourselves to be captured. If the American soldier comes, kill him, and then cut your own throat.

For some reason I had no fear from this training. Because I simply thought that Japan was going to win the war. It never really occurred to me that we could actually be conquered, that American soldiers would ever set foot in Yatsushiro! Yatsushiro was Japan and Japan was God's Country.

But one day I was sitting in class and I eyed a globe. It had never really interested me before, because the world beyond my village never really mattered. With the beginning of the war, though, all these strange places like America began to seem like living creatures—like the eels or octopus in my father's shop. I wanted to give them shape and size. That's when I got the shock of my life up to then. I turned the globe after looking at Japan and saw America. Japan seemed like a sardine, America like a whale. It was huge! The country seemed to take one whole side of the sphere while tiny Japan was just a sliver. I had to share my epiphany with someone so I rushed straight home that night and talked to my mother.

"How can we ever beat this huge country," I asked her. "Have you seen how big America is?"

She shuddered and grew pale. I can still see her face today. "You watch your mouth," she said sternly to me. "If the thought police find out about this, they're going to take you away."

When the war with America began, there was little that changed at first. Obviously all the news we were getting spoke of our great victories abroad, and how God's Country would soon triumph. But it became clear over the next year that life was changing for the worse in my country. At the business school, we were drafted to work in the local alcohol factory—the largest employer, and the most strategic asset, in Yatsushiro. Japan was resource poor that was why we invaded Asia, for its access to oil.

CHAPTER 8

A Battle

But as the war wore on, we were losing that resource, and alcohol was used to fuel everything. Soon, all private businesses were shut down as the government took over food production. The fish market was closed, and because of my father's well-known status, he was put in charge of the cafeteria and food distribution at the factory. It was a job he was well suited for, because all of his black market skills came into play. Even as things grew rough, we lived better than most thanks to my father. My mother shared as much as we could, too, and I think that helped us out when things got rough later for everyone. Many people remembered the generosity of my mother.

My father's generosity was more problematical. As smoothly as he ran the black markets of the town, he was less successful in managing the underworld of his love life. As the war began, rationing took a hard bite out of everyone, especially his elaborate franchising arrangements with his wives. Aunt Toshi's franchise was no longer needed, so my father brought her to work selling fish in front of our house.

The fish store was the center of distribution for rationing, so everyone in the village came to pick up their allotment, including Wives Two, Three and Four. But since Hideichi's mother had married, the obnoxious Aunt Toshi, was now wife Number Two, and this caused problems with my mother, who resented the fact that she had to share any revenue with these women. When times were good, the wives' extra income helped everyone. But now they were a drain on my mother's lifestyle, and the tension between my parents was growing. Father handled the situation by keeping them both at a distance, but one day Aunt Toshi showed up to fetch her fish while my mother was conveniently away. In one of those rare moments of letting his guard down, father invited her into our house and told her to make some tea.

Just then my mother returned, and entered her sacred kitchen to find this horrid shrew casing her wares. The two women began screaming even as Toshi retreated through the house, the fish shop, and into the street. As she turned to walk away, my mother wouldn't stop. She followed along, yelling, and slapping her on the back. She just seemed to get angrier and angrier, and she wouldn't stop slapping Aunt Toshi.

"You bitch, you dirty bitch. What are you doing in my house," my mother screamed at her.

Toshi was almost running, but then she stopped, turned around and slapped my mother. Before anybody could react, the two had flipped over a table and were wrestling in the middle of the street.

A crowd gathered and my father, just down the street talking to some friends, noticed the uproar outside. The other storekeepers seemed shocked. Nobody had seen such a thing—two respectable women fighting in the street—so they didn't really know what to do. Father lunged through the crowd and tried to separate the two women. I just stood there crying. I was frightened and embarrassed. Some people continued walked, trying to ignore it, because they didn't want to embarrass my father. But the crowd shifted back and forth as the two women fell and rolled all over the narrow street.

In terms of physicality, the walrus-sized Aunt Toshi was,

overwhelmingly, the stronger of the two. And what's more she looked really frightening. In all my eight years I'd never seen anyone look so angry. She advanced on my mother, froth bubbling at the corners of her mouth. Crying, I yelled encouragement at my mother, "C'mon, mama. Don't give up. You can do it." My mother was - no matter who you were and how you looked at it - the more beautiful of the two women. So here was this beautiful woman — who many other women were jealous of — squabbling with her husband's fat, ugly mistress. You can understand the attraction on a typically boring day in rural Japan.

Toshi Oba-san was heavier, but my mother seemed stronger. She held her own, probably because she had the wrath of a scorned woman on her side. Soon, because they really couldn't get a grip on each other, they were pulling each other's hair trying to swing the other into tables and doorposts. Neither would let up so they just swung around in a widening circle as people tried to dodge them. My father, with the help of the apprentices, finally got the two women separated. Toshi, her dress torn and her face scratched, was breathing heavily and looked like she was going to faint. My mother was still angry and probably would have killed her if she could. Toshi picked up her rations and left. My father pulled my mother into the house and slapped her hard. It was the only time I ever saw my father hit anybody.

The Higher Thought Police, or the *Kempeitai*, patrolled our village throughout the war. They were the Japanese equivalent of the German SS, the Chinese Red Guards or any other strong arm of a totalitarian government. They were frightening and had the power to lock you up, destroy your life, and perhaps even end it if you crossed them. They were outsiders, too—Japanese from other parts of the country—so they had no respect for any of the local powers or customs. With dark green uniforms, high black boots and sabers that always rattled when they walk, these young men were always on the lookout for spies or any signs of security violations. We workers dressed in gray, which seemed a lowly color at the time. The *kempeitai* would search us at the end of every shift. Since there was so little to eat, people would try to steal whatever they could get their hands on. They had children, and those children needed food, and every day, it seemed someone was caught trying to steal and beaten right there at the gates of the factory. I don't know how anybody succeeded in fooling these soldiers, but I know my father would smuggle out sugar and then take it to the countryside where he'd trade for eggs and other produce. Since he ran the black market, which exploded under wartime rationing, he had to bend over backward to keep these guys happy. He did it by giving them the best sugar, eggs, rice, fish, and alcohol he skimmed off the top of every shipment he received. He buttered them up, flattered their egos, and made them laugh.

The factory was a key asset in the town, and that made it a target along with other factories. I worked in the accounting department, handling the books with other students and adult clerks. They had put me there because I was very good with the abacus in doing calculations. In addition to the Japanese, we had about 50 young Korean men, essentially war slaves, who worked at the factory. We weren't supposed to talk to these men, but my father felt sorry for them and often gave them extra food. They performed many different jobs, and were essentially no different than the Japanese workers, but they were at much greater risk. Paranoia was second nature in our society, and any foreigner or Japanese with foreign ties was at great risk. In my own business school we had a Taiwanese student who was completely shunned by the class because of fears he might be a spy.

Among the Koreans I remember best was a kind, gentle man

named Mr. Takeda. *Takeda-san* frequently delivered items to the office where I worked, and though it was forbidden, we often struck up a conversation. He had a Japanese name because Japanese had been made the required language in Korea, which Japan conquered and colonized in 1905. I think my father took a liking to Takeda mainly because his oldest son was in the war, and he missed him so. Takeda reminded him of my brother.

About two years after the war with America began, sometime in 1943, B-29s began appearing regularly over Yatsushiro. To an awe-struck young girl, they seemed like magical silver ships sweeping in and out and out of the clouds, flying low you could easily identify their markings. They didn't immediately bomb us, because Yatsushiro didn't offer any important targets. But as the war continued, the explosions seemed to grow closer and closer. Soon, the planes were flying low enough to fire their machine guns at our towns back and forth from their real missions.

Everyone had a bomb shelter dug into the floor, beneath the tatami mat. Yatsushiro had two targets that might be considered strategic—the alcohol factory and a large cement factory that sat near the center of town. We all realized that our turn would come soon.

Food became scarce, and many families sent their children to the remote countryside both to protect them from the bombing, and in the hope that they could find vegetables at the source, on farms and in rivers and forests. There was severe rationing and simply no food to eat. As the war continued, harvest seasons had been missed and fishing disrupted. Our roads and cities were cratered and gutted. Everywhere there was a factory or the possibility of a military base, there was wreckage. People were gaunt, frail, and sick. Children were starving, and the elderly were dying before their time. There were many who killed themselves, people who were just too depressed or overwhelmed with what everyone knew was a colossal defeat. This was how it was felt in a small town, far from Tokyo. Everyone had assumed victory, believed what they were told. With defeat, there were no longer any illusions to sustain their minds over their starving bodies. The value of paper money was worthless. People bartered because money was worthless. They emptied their houses of clothes and furniture and tools and just carted them from town to town looking to trade for food. You would see men and woman bent over with huge piles of clothes tied over their backs, just stumbling along the sides of roads. I remember at one point I was visiting a friend and her mother gave me an egg. They owned a chicken and regularly ate boiled eggs. I had never tasted an egg—it was a luxury back then—and it was so wonderful. I had tears in my eyes. Like everyone, I was always very hungry and nothing tasted so wonderful as that egg. But was over so quickly.

This situation continued until well after the war was over. We kept hearing rumors that McArthur was coming. I felt that I was going to be killed because we had no information. We had been trained to kill Americans with the bamboo spears, so you can understand why we were all very confused. If they showed up now, should we still kill them? Should we just kill ourselves? And what would these Americans do? Rape us? Kill us? Turn us into slaves? I cried a lot. I really believed my short life was coming to an end. We had always been a poor country, at least in the Japan where I grew up, so you can understand how confused we were. I never felt part of a great nation, and now I didn't realize how defeated we might be.

CHAPTER 9

The Bomb

The day they dropped the atomic bomb on Nagasaki, the earth shook in Yatsushiro. The ancient city of Nagasaki was far on the other side of Kyushu from our village, and few had ever been there. Still, on Kyushu, it was an important center of learning and trade, and more importantly, one of the first sites of contact between Japan and the early Western explorers. The few Christian churches in Japan were in Nagasaki. Destroying it was an important symbolic step to defeating our people.

I was at Taiyo elementary school that day. Everybody gathered in a field next to the school whenever the air raid sirens went off, just to stay away from the danger. It had become a reflex, and since the sirens were now sounding all the time, more and more people just went there each day as the war progressed. I don't know how this practice started, but I guess people thought that the Americans wouldn't bomb a school, or strafe so many civilians standing alone in a field. A huge oak tree dominated the field. It was hundreds of years old and had a huge hole in the middle, like a cave. Generations of children in the village grew up playing around it and climbing inside the hole.

We had no idea what was happening with the war, and there was so much fear of the secret police that few people even discussed it openly. What we did notice was that instead of flying alone, the B-29s were increasingly flying in V formations, like flocks of birds. We had never seen that before. I'm sure to the smarter adults this new sight didn't signal victory. After all, if the Americans were so dominating our skies that they could cover them in planes, how could Japan be winning? I didn't know what to make of it, though, and each day just became a routine of going to the schoolyard, staring up into the sky, listening to the bombs exploding, and milling about with the other townspeople.

August 9th began like any other day until that explosion, the one that destroyed Nagasaki. None of us had heard of the bombing of Hiroshima, just a few days before. It wasn't reported on the radio, of course. And nobody had heard of an atomic bomb. We all knew the sounds of the regular bombs, and of the guns strafing the area from various American planes. But the Nagasaki blast was something of a whole other magnitude, like an earthquake. Suddenly, just around noon, the entire earth shook and then a huge blinding light engulfed the horizon. It was beautiful, a luscious orange turning whiter that highlighted our faces, like a celestial flashbulb but growing slowly and lasting much longer. Then we saw the mushroom cloud, just unfolding over the trees as some kind of gigantic living sculpture. You could see anything in it you wanted. It was only much later that the facts came out, that the true horror of the event we witnessed became clear. At least 74,000 people died instantly in the cloud that we stood staring at.

We were rapt, as if in a trance, all staring in the same direction shocked but also awed at the sight. The explosion and its sound lasted for an hour it seemed, but the cloud was with us for the rest of the day. At some point, though, people eventually went home. Did they know it signaled defeat? Maybe on some unconscious level, but I can't say anyone voiced it openly. That night, people huddled, and murmured nonsense just to say something. The adults just had to speak, talk to each other, just to remind themselves they were still alive.

A week later, on August 15th, an announcement came over the radio that the Emperor was going to be speaking to the nation. That was the end, and everyone knew it. Nobody had to wait to hear the emperor because they knew such an event—he had never spoken publicly—could only mean we had lost the war. All of the old people were crying, crammed in tight circles around their radios. Then their sons and daughters started wailing, and soon even I was crying though I didn't know why. People were rolling on the ground, and some screamed. Everywhere you looked. The elders were in shock because they had been raised to think of this man as a living embodiment of God. That idea had weakened among the younger generations, but there was still much emotion connected to this man. All of these people had a son, a daughter, a brother or a sister who had suffered so much because of this so-called god. When he came on the radio, I remember the sounds but could not understand the language—it was a rarefied, ancient Japanese that few younger people understood. Some of the grandparents, though, could make out what he was saying and translated for the rest of us. The worst was confirmed, and everybody seemed in a daze. Most people didn't move, for days it seemed. We just walked around as if in a trance. The most apparent change was that the *kempeitai* had fled. They just disappeared over night, leaving their uniforms scattered all over the place. They knew that the people would come for them first, especially after enduring years of beating in the factory and on the streets. The beatings had increased as sugar, alcohol, and rice had become ever more rare, and I had witnessed many of these clubbings and sword whippings at the factory gates when workers were discovered with stolen supplies.

Most of the *kempeitai* were not from our area, and I'm sure they returned to their own villages.

In the weeks that followed you'd hear many stories of elderly people killing themselves around the village. It seemed to be happening every day. Nobody I knew, but each death was the subject of sad conversation between my father and the other men at the fish shop.

Were the Americans coming to kill us? No one knew. We had been trained to expect the worst, and to fight to the death. But now we had been told by our god that Japan was defeated. What did that mean? Should we still die with honor, or prepare for lives as slaves, much like the Koreans who we had made our slaves? Our only knowledge of the Americans had been as decadent, selfish corrupt people, with foul manners, no traditions and few achievements. Barbarians.

CHAPTER 10

A Brighter Future

Then one day—things just seemed to happen overnight back then—you started hearing stories that Americans were good and kind, that they didn't want to kill us but actually wanted to rebuild Japan. We had been so brainwashed. Little by little food began to appear in the market. Buildings were being erected, and roads cleared up. You could start finding fish and produce again.

I started taking dancing lessons again. I had studied traditional Japanese dance since I was 6, but I began getting serious about it with the encouragement of my new instructor. I started to learn after being inspired by photos that I saw of *maiko-san*, the apprentice geisha girls of Kyoto. The tradition in the village at the time was that the daughters of all the fish merchants took traditional dance lessons so that they could be on display during seasonal festivals. This also told the rest of the village that the family was prosperous enough to afford sending their girls to dance masters. But I always loved dance more than just a hobby, and I thought I was good enough at it to someday become a teacher or professional. I loved the way it made me feel, the precision of the movements, the feeling of the blood coursing through me after several hours of practice, the sense that I was a part of something much greater than my tedious life in the village.

This didn't sit well with my father, who felt that a life in the arts of any kind was going to be useless in our shattered country. He had long struggled with my love of dance—he had forbid me for a while to take lessons after I did poorly on my exams. He especially became enraged at one point when I told him I wanted to become a geisha, and move to Kyoto. I was bonkura, after all, and who would ever want to marry a stupid dancer, especially one going around advertising she wanted to be a geisha! And who had the time to watch someone dance or sing when they were starving? Especially in a backwater like Yatsushiro.

This from a guy who practically lived with geishas, not to mention half the women of the region. Of course there was a double standard, and it enraged me, but it was still incredibly naïve of me to compare myself to my father. And extremely radical. Here the leading fishmonger of the village has to deal with this daughter who thinks she can be as powerful as him someday.

Japanese traditional dance, or *Nihon buyo,* is an offshoot of Kabuki theater. It developed because it provided women an outlet, since females are not allowed to perform in traditional Kabuki productions. The *buyo-ka*, or dancer, perfects the daily gestures of Japanese culture, from a simple act like drinking rice wine, or moving across a stage. Everything ripples through your body, from your first breath to your final shudder, is practiced and refined over and over again. The pelvis must be set just right, and the knees bent correctly. The idea is basically a series of stylized movements that look good when wearing a kimono.

The movement of the hem of a kimono looks awful if you walk with big strides. In order to walk in the smooth, sliding style that looks good with a kimono, you have to bend slightly at the hips and keep the knees bent slightly. Everything is practiced, from the wearing of the kimono and walking in *tabi* footwear, to how to fold and put away these items. There are five main schools of this dance, and the two that I was learning under were the Fujima and the Hanayagi schools—these are the original names of the masters who developed these dance forms during the Edo Period of Japan's history hundreds of years ago.

Katsuko wearing a Kimono

In Japan, once a teacher masters the technique, he takes on the name of the school. Thus my instructors in Yatsushiro were Fujima Koishi and Hanayagi Kotaro, her husband. They were both wonderful, very nice, warm people. But in the studio they were extremely stern, always serious. Hanayagi was a tall, thin, very handsome man. If you dressed him up like a samurai, he had the grace and poise to be a movie star. He was from Osaka, which is the center of the theater world in Japan, and had all the wit of Osakan people in their rich dialect. His wife was quieter, being a product of Yatsushiro, but always gracious when she discussed her craft.

CHAPTER 11

First Love

Their studio was a sanctuary for me, and the place that I embarked on the next chapter of my life, the one that would carry me through heartache but ultimately out of the village and into the city. I met the first true love of my life, a seemingly quiet young ex-soldier named *Masunori Eguchi*. One day I noticed him talking to my instructor, who introduced us. Later, I had heard a rumor that he had been a member of what came to be known as the kamikazes, so I went up to him and asked him about it. He told me his entire story right there on the spot.

Masunori had been trained as a kamikaze pilot, but the war had ended before his opportunity for death and it had scarred him. We didn't call them kamizaze at the time—they were *tokubetsu kogeki tai* (special attack units), or *tokkotai.* Like all of us, those who grew up in the wartime system, he had been brainwashed to believe that dying for Japan was glorious. During the last years of the war, the slogan *Jusshi Reisho*—Sacrifice Life—was drilled into us. We were all kamikazes in a sense, and we were all going through a type of post-traumatic stress of conflicted feelings as we tried to rebuild new lives out of the rubble all around us. For us, the young people, it was probably much easier than those whose best years lay behind in the ruins. We had a chance to build a new country and a new life. But it would be too late before I realized just how much Masunori was marred by his experience—a promised sacrifice that failed. At the time I was taken with the romance of it all.

Like his friends, Masunori came of fighting age just as Japan's overwhelming defeat became apparent to us all. The best pilots had long ago died. Oil was scarce. The parts for planes were rapidly disappearing. Children were being trained for future aerial combat by strapping them into bamboo wheels and spinning them until they were sick. This was supposed to simulate flight!

The Americans surrounded us and bombing runs were a daily fact of life. Instead of surrender, the fascists who ruled us decided to sacrifice students who could barely fly. Those who actually climbed into planes were only taught to take off and maneuver—after all, they only had to live long enough to plunge into enemy ships. Our leaders honestly believed that by sending a generation of young men to die that this was somehow not a defeat, but a step towards victory. It was said that those who died for the emperor would be praised at the famous Yasukuni Shrine and would be happy forever in the afterlife. The generals seemed to think that by showing the fanaticism of their youth, they would somehow kill the Americans' spirit.

The tokkotai set off on their mission from my home island of Kyushu. After taking Okinawa, the Americans were supposed to come up through Kyushu, the southernmost of Japan's original islands, on a bloody march to Tokyo. For that reason, the tokkotai were trained and departed from places on our island like the base at Kagoshima at the southwest tip of the island. Those like Masunori who were chosen were not forced, but only subtly urged to sacrifice their lives for the fatherland. They filled out questionnaires in which they were asked whether they "desired earnestly" or merely "wished" to be involved in kamikaze attacks. There was great pressure on these young men to circle one of these two answers, but the army only selected those who circled the first. But there were so many volunteers that only those with the best grades went first. Once accepted, they were put in a rigorous program that kept them continuously busy from sunup to sunrise, so they'd never have a chance to reconsider their dire choice.

Masunori was a member of a group of tokkotai based in Kanoya in Kagoshima. He had been scheduled to pilot a 'Zero' fighter plane one final time in mid-August, 1945. As the clock ticked down to that fateful day, Masunori's friends took off before him, one by one. There was no alcohol left by that time so as Masunori and his fellow pilots lined up to bid their comrades farewell, they toasted them with cups of water: "For Japan. For the Emperor. Banzai, banzai, banzai."

The young kamikaze pilots wore bandanas wrapped around their foreheads as they climbed into their cockpits. They waved to the comrades as they took off. In reply, those waving them off would say, "We shall be right behind you."

Masunori had seen so many of his friends fly off to die. He had risen through the three-year program, but he had not yet graduated to his final flight. Masunori had been told his death would come on Aug. 18, 1945. But on Aug. 15, Emperor Hirohito announced the surrender over the radio. A wave of hysteria instantly swept through the ranks of these young men. Every one had spent more than a year preparing for certain death. It influenced every breath they took, every meal they ate, every letter they wrote home to their mothers and fathers. Masunori had been trained to follow them, and he had failed.

A group of pilots that Masunori knew got together on a cliff and leapt to their deaths. Others decided to kill themselves by seppuku—slicing open their bellies with their military swords while a comrade beheaded them. Masunori did not follow them. He told me he had thought long and hard about killing himself, but had felt torn between his loyalty to his friends and his duty to his mother. His father had died long ago. She was old and alone and there were no other children to take care of her. He would be killing her, too, and that held no honor.

So he drifted for a while, battling with his guilt and other demons. But gradually he returned to acting, his first love, and began studying all elements of the craft, including traditional dance. His dream was to have his own acting troupe that would travel from town to town entertaining the defeated Japanese. He had ended up in Yatsushiro as an apprentice at my dance instructor's studio.

When I heard his story, obviously I was swept off my feet. We began seeing each other a lot. He had moved into the teacher's house about a month before I had begun my lessons. He was very passionate about dancing.

I think I felt a little sorry for him, protective maybe in that way women are around needy men, because of all that he had been through. Life had been tough for everyone, of course, but a defeated army still held a special place in our hearts. We had suffered much on the home front, but the stories that returned with those who survived suggested a horror even we could not imagine. There were tales of starvation, cannibalism, disease, and unimaginable barbarity beneath the American bombs.

We had so much in common, especially the sheer love of stagecraft—the singing, dancing, costume-making, and the illusion of performance. He was a masterful dancer, and would have made an excellent master. He had begun studying before the war—his father was a naval captain, so he came from a very good family before his father died, plunging his mother into poverty. We were very much influenced by American Broadway, what was known of it and smuggled into Japan. Our plays were a hodgepodge of traditional Japanese theater and American style epics. I wrote the plays, simple stories of Samurai derring-do, and Romeo and Juliet type love stories. We put on the huge wigs, and the old-style kimonos and performed wherever anybody would watch us around Yatsushiro. A bit of this was on the sly, since we were not permitted to put on plays not sanctioned by the master of the school. He always preferred that we study the old style drama, Kabuki and Nihon buyo.

CHAPTER 12

Elopement

My father got angry when he heard about my boyfriend. People heard what was going on and started spreading rumors. In a small town everybody knows your business. The guy wasn't from Yatsushiro, and that was a big concern since father didn't know his family at all. Japanese courtship is rooted very much in the idea of the group—you don't marry an individual, you marry his family. You marry his entire line. You marry his profession, and the profession of his father and grandfather. A male dancer, of all things, just wasn't a respectable source of income. And they were rootless, since being an actor at that time meant traveling from town to town. They were *Floating Weeds*, as the title of the famous Ozu film about actors suggests. It was shocking, in fact, and suggested the same sexual laxity and confusion that it would even today in some quarters. That's why even today in Japan investigators are hired to scrutinize records and family trees going back generations to weed out scandal, untouchables (those who work in the leather trades) or even worse, hidden Koreans. He was an outsider and a dancer at that! Father had a hard time with the idea of a failed kamikaze turned dancer wooing his only daughter. He wanted me to get married to somebody in the fish business.

Father would tell me, "I can't let you marry somebody weak, feminine. I don't even want to meet him." My father was very stubborn.

No meant no.

We had been dating for about six months. We knew that we wanted to be together, and we knew that it was never going to happen in Yatsushiro. So we decided to elope. We planned this out secretly, but it was clear that our intentions were leaking out. My father suspected. I knew because he started saying no to everything whenever I needed money or wanted to go out somewhere.

But I was just as headstrong, and reckless. The idea of a 19-year-old girl in such a conservative place as Yatsushiro doing such a thing was unheard of. I suspected things like this happened, but it was very rare. Even worse than the sexual aspect, it suggested selfishness, an insult to your father and family, a slap to your tribe. You never heard about such behavior, because often the woman was disowned, banished. And the family acted as if she had never existed. Disgrace such as this would send you deep into the water trade, as a prostitute.

But we didn't care. Maybe it was because so much of our society, our culture, had been destroyed and discredited by the war. The system had failed our generation and so much had suffered for it. We were going to live the life that we chose. As another sign of disrespect, Masunori was taking steps to form his own company, perform his own plays, break away from his master. He had started his own company—*Hanai Kenoske*—which was his stage name.

Because of all that we did, our teacher got a bad reputation. The master, realizing that we were not turning back, tried to see my dad to explain the situation to him. But my father was having none of it, and only grew angrier at his attempts to ease the tension. Hanayagi Kotaro was also worried that his name would be destroyed when we eloped.

I grew to hate my father at this point. I couldn't stand to be around him any longer and I had to get out of Yatsushiro. The sooner, the better. I felt I had been mistreated all my life at that point. I had wasted my childhood looking for him, chasing down his mistresses and wives. Treated like an apprentice, and dressed like a boy. I felt bad living in such a family, embarrassed. None of my friends had such a family. I just wanted out.

I don't really think I loved Masunori as much as I saw him as my ticket out of Yatsushiro. As bold as my decision was, for a woman to leave town alone would have been virtually impossible. Then I truly would have been regarded as a prostitute.

In the end, we were simply forced out. The talk grew too loud, and the tension between my friends, my family and my dance master, grew too strong.

We left in the middle of the day, a cold rainy autumn day in which I did more crying than the skies. The banks of the Kuma River had swelled and the streets were filled with mud. People seemed to be walked carefully around me, almost as if they sensed my fragility, but it was only to dodge the deep puddles. I had poured my heart out to Masunori, begging him to take me away from this bleak life. We walked along the banks of the river, then huddled for a while in the courtyard of a shrine. We talked, hugged,cried, and made our final decision.

When I think back to this time, I can only remember my anger. It clouds all, the uncertain feelings I had for Masunori, the train ride out of the village. I so hated my dad because I had worked hard and looked up to him so long. I hated my mother for putting up with this charismatic, handsome, dishonest man. I hated her for letting jealousy consume her, for not standing up to him, his wives, or his relatives. I thought my father loved me above all, that I was special. I thought we had a bond because of all those mornings I had gone to fetch him, and the interest I had showed in his craft. I was hurt and angry. I thought he should have understood me above all, but he never did.

It was one hour by train to Minamata. The town had sustained serious damage, far more devastating than Yatsushiro. The fields around the town were all burned. The buildings were piles of rubble. The entire town, in fact, was just one continuous line of broken wood, shattered concrete and heaps of garbage. The streets were just paths cleared in the middle of this destruction. I was shocked because this was really my first look at the outside world. There had been a strategic factory in the town. It made fertilizer, the strategic ingredients of which also went to the manufacture of explosives. The Americans had bombed it over and over again. By the time I walked through these streets, I wasn't angry, I wasn't sad. I was perhaps as emotionally numb as those who had sustained these bombings. I was completely open to what the future would bring. I wasn't fearful because I didn't really see that I had any choice. Since my father was opposed to what I wanted to do, I didn't see any future for me in Yatsushiro.

The poverty was immense in Minamata and I only slowly began to realize, that though I had never thought of myself as rich, my father's power and privilege in Yatsushiro had put me in what might be called the upper middle class back then. Masunori's mother lived in a simple, poorly constructed house that leaned to the left. Once they had been prosperous – Masunori's father was a well-to-do shipping agent. But then he died, leaving behind no insurance, or safety net. So great was their plight that they couldn't even afford to feed themselves, and Masunori's older brother had been adopted by relatives to relieve the burden. That left no one to care for Kishi-san but Masunori in this small, decrepit hovel. The wood was wet and rotting, and every day the smell of human waste was strong. They were using their own feces as fertilizer in the fields, and it permeated everything. Everyone around was poor and I had never seen such poverty, even during the worst days of the War in Yatsushiro. My tiny village was a city compared to this place.

Later, Minamata would become a worldwide symbol of environmental horror when mercury poisoning killed hundreds and deformed an entire generation of newborn children. The town faces the Shiranui Sea, and Minamata Bay is part of this sea. The fertilizer company that dominated Minamata, the Chisso Corporation, had dumped this mercury into the bay beginning in the 1930s and had paid off the fisherman to keep quiet as habitats in the bay and surrounding sea were destroyed. Especially after the war, the factory was the only real source of livelihoods. But even if the people didn't sell the fish, they caught and ate it themselves as the only food they could afford. The surrounding beaches often smelled of dead fish and rotting birds, and an acrid pall of smog hung over the town on many days.

In the 1950s, people began talking of a strange disease in Minamata. Limbs lost their feeling and shriveled, people began acting crazy and suicides increased. Babies were born horribly deformed. It was all in the water. I probably drank my share, and I'm very lucky that the child I later gave birth to in this horrid place was not stricken himself. But these horrors were not revealed until much later, and I can only say that when I learned of them, based on what I witnessed there, I was not surprised.

CHAPTER 13

Life Away from Home

Masunori's house had only two rooms, and the tatami mat on the floor was old and frayed. In a few places it had worn through and the dirt floor was soft and wet, like a wound. The roof was made of straw and it leaked during heavy rains. I remember spreading pots to catch water all over the house nearly every day during the rainy season. He had never told me how poor his family was. Perhaps he was ashamed.

What had I done coming here? That thought did cross my mind in a matter of hours, despite my love for Masunori and the heady mix of fear and wonder at finally fleeing Yatsushiro.

His mother, *Kishi-san*, was indeed small, old and frail, and bent so severely from bad bones that you had to bend just to talk to her. Her back was so bent that it was a wonder that her head didn't scrape the floor. Despite this Kishi-san would still shoulder a bucket-yoke full of fertilizer and walk for thirty minutes or more to the field where she grew a variety of tubers and vegetables. She was probably about sixty years old when I met her but she looked ninety. But she had a bright, welcoming smile, and she soon became a second mother to me. Her kindness was all the more important because she was truly shocked when we arrived at her broken door. Though she wasn't angry, she was concerned about the feelings of my parents, and asked how they felt about what we were doing. Her son had never written her about me, or warned that we were coming there to live with her.

I was honest. I told her that my father was against the union, but that I felt her son was the right man for me. I can understand why they feel that way, she said. But she never said a harsh word to me from that point on.

I can't stress how much I was shocked to be living in such a house. The structure sat less than a dozen yards off the beach, and at night you'd hear the roar of the surf. Fishing boats would be lined up on the beach, and the clean salt air was ruined by the smell of rotting fish, shit, and gasoline. It was an unbelievable smell—you just don't smell things like that any more in Japan. There was no kitchen. You had to cook and prepare food outside, in the early morning and the late evening, beneath the stars. It was a struggle just to open the door to enter the house. There was the dirty floor and two clay ovens, mainly used for heat. The inside walls were burned black because of the heat of the ovens. And there was no chimney, so the smell of shit was only overcome by the smell of smoke. The toilet was uncovered, and if it was raining and your control was poor, you'd be soaked. The bathtub was also out in the middle of the field, so a woman could only clean herself in the dark and hope that no stranger happened upon her. There was straw hanging from one wall of the house and at first I didn't know what it was for. But that was the toilet paper. You cleaned yourself with the straw and then used it as fertilizer, so as not to waste anything. The only luxury was a faucet, oddly enough. The village had some kind of internal plumbing, so I never had to pump water. A small step up for me. His family survived by farming a small plot, far from the house, in the mountains, where they grew sweet potatoes for market. His mother would sling the sack of fertilizer over her sloping shoulder—it was way too heavy for me, at first—and hike up the mountain to farm the tiny plot. Later, though,

I grew stronger and could carry the fertilizer—our own excrement that we'd piled into bags—up into the mountains.

We stayed there about two months, trying to figure out our next step. Masunori got a job in a nearby factory, and that provided enough money to eat. But we had our dreams, and we were wary about getting locked into the life of a place even more isolated and numbing than Yatsushiro. So one day we set off and traveled to Nagashima Island in Kagoshima Prefecture, on the southern tip of Kyushu and made our rounds of the small villages scattered around the region. Our day was usually spent pulling into a town and then handing out flyers, banging our ceremonial drums, and alerting people in the fields and surrounding hamlets that there would be a show that night. We would perform several shows in a clearing, perhaps a public park or the village square, if it still existed, that night, then begin the whole process over again the next day.

The audience would sit on the floor of whatever space we found, bringing their own straw mattresses. What buildings were left after the bombing in most places could not be spared for theater work. Kagoshima was hit particularly hard, because it was the site of a major naval base, and plans for the abandoned invasion of the home islands would have started in Kyushu, and worked north up through the islands. In many towns, you'd look across a horizon of debris.

There were many small villages in Kagoshima Prefecture. We traveled by rickshaw from town to town with our costumes, instruments, and other gear. Our shows were very heightened melodrama, with lots of swashbuckling and swordplay. They usually involved samurais or noble Yakuzas, the denizens of the Japanese criminal gangs. You might think Seven Samurai—ne're-do-wells who suddenly decide they are going to save peasants being oppressed by cruel landlords. You have to remember, especially outside the major cities, there wasn't much competition for entertainment. And people were feeling defeated, depressed by years of failed government, dead sons and defeated armies. Typically, about 20 people would show up for each performance, which was quite good given the size of many of the villages. Sometimes women would protest that there wasn't much romance, but these were mainly men who went to these shows, and they didn't' want romance, or fancy dancing. They wanted action, just as most men do today. They wanted to see the strong protect the weak peasants, like many of them.

We literally worked for food. The price of admission was some rice, potatoes, maybe a tool or a piece of clothing—whatever the villagers wanted to barter. We certainly weren't going to grow rich doing this and I can't honestly say I knew what the goal was. I harbored no dreams of becoming a great actress, or a geisha anymore, or of even having my own dance studio someday. I had no dreams at all. I was still going through the shock of separation from my family. My body seemed be changing, and I was often very moody. I threw up a lot.

CHAPTER 14

With Child

I was pregnant. Since life was hard on the road, and hauling rickshaws from village to village put a lot of stress on your back, Masunori sent me back home to stay with his mother. He was as shocked as I was that I was going to have a baby, but he really didn't show any emotion. At least until he knew it was a boy. That was simply the way men acted back then. Having a child was women's work and they didn't concern themselves with it. His mother and I would spend our days farming their small plot, or bartering for fish, rice and other food in the nearby markets. We'd then go fishing for oysters on the beach, and combine them with a potato to make our daily soup. Farming had been devastated by much of the bombing, and rice was still a luxury, so soup was usually all we had to eat.

Despite her many maladies, Kishi-san had the energy and drive of an ox. She would still shoulder a bucket-yoke full of fertilizer and walk for thirty minutes or more to the field where she grew a variety of tubers and vegetables.

"Mother-in-law," I'd say to her, "I'll help you." Kishi-san would just laugh me off, saying, "You're from a good family, so I bet you've never done this sort of work before, have you?"

At night, I would bathe Kishi-san, wash her hunched back and brush her long, thinning hair. She was in her last years, clearly, and much of her hair would comb out in small clumps. He'd make it back to see me every few weeks, and gradually brought the troupe to perform closer to Minamata. We still were not officially married—there were no government offices to register a marriage or even a new birth. And I had not had any contact with my family for months. But feeling a bit scared and lonely, I decided the least I would do was contact my father and tell him that he would soon be a grandfather. I wrote a letter to him describing my life up to that point. I received a reply quickly, in a matter of days, saying that he wanted to come visit me. He arrived and met me at the house of the local fish baron, who seemed to think it was a great honor that Takenaga of Yatsushiro was coming to visit him in tiny Minamata. He only realized when my father arrived that he was there to see me. The man was shocked to learn that Takenaga's daughter was living in scandal in a leaning house in Minamata.

When my father saw me, he just cried. I was in my last month and no amount of clothing could hide my condition. Still, I was shocked at his running tears. I had never seen such emotion from this rough man. We didn't say much. He didn't offer help, and I didn't ask for any, despite my desperate situation. We parted formally, almost like casual friends saying goodbye.

My child was born on July 30, 1948, just as the sun was sinking into the waves. I was alone with an old woman. Masunori was off performing somewhere. It was a rough delivery, but his mother and later, a local midwife, were with me every step of the way.

I wailed loudly throughout the birth. As I lay there agonizing, a flurry of thoughts swirled around inside my head: I hadn't been able to see a doctor before the birth; the surrounding area was teeming with lice; all of my clothes were at the pawnshop and I didn't have anything decent to change into. Never had I thought to bring a child into the world in such an environment and I wept with anguish at the thought. All I recall hearing now is the waves lapping up on the beach behind us broken only by my screams, then the cry of my son. I named the boy *Kazunori*.

Masunori was away performing for much of the time after Kazunori was born. He was becoming ever more distant from his mother, the child, and me. I would only learn later why he seemed so intent on staying away. And when he did return I began seeing a darker side of him. He drank hard—that was true of many Japanese men at this time—but the alcohol seemed to unleash demons that had stayed hidden on the road and in Yatsushiro. He undoubtedly was still marked by his experiences during the war, but I think he was also feeling the pressures of being a small artist in a time and place that really had no patience with art. Money was always tight, and it was just easier for him to escape his multiplying duties and bleak home life whenever he could. The rages grew, and he began to beat me. At first, they were just small outbursts. But as time went on they became as regular as daybreak, and I came to expect them. There was never enough money, and certainly never enough money for drink. Even more dangerous was the strong, homemade stuff he might find in a backward place like Minamata. Drinking that would not only create an addiction, but do serious brain damage to a man already so damaged.

CHAPTER 15

Hard Times

Every day came with a new demand that I make more money while he was away acting. When these demands first began, I was in my last months and the beatings were especially hard. He never hit me in the stomach, but he slapped me hard across the face, until I was as purple and swollen as a blowfish. I had no clue how I was going to earn anything in such a small place. So his attention turned to my belongings, the precious dresses and theater clothes I had accumulated over the years. This was more than just a wardrobe—it was a hobby, a keepsake, a way of life for me. The idea of selling them was almost like selling the child in my womb.

But sell them I did, in the hope that they'd end the beatings. Picture me: very pregnant, tired, probably smelling of fish and shit, hauling kimonos in a rickshaw to the local pawn shop. Whenever I refused, he'd destroy the tiny house, breaking the furniture and throwing whatever he could hurl at me. I was afraid the whole rickety house would come down if he hit the right spot with a metal pot. His mother would try to protect my stomach, but he'd slap at her too. Whenever he tried to hit her, I'd then put myself in front of her. It must have seemed comical to watch, two women, each trying to protect the other, each trying to shove the other away and draw the beating of their abuser. I'd beg him to stop, especially from breaking our furniture and plates, since it was all we had. It was the plates, not the blows, that I worried about most. A bruise would always heal, but a plate was too expensive to replace. Rice, fish, dishes—he'd send them sailing all over the tiny house. And I'd try to sweep up and save whatever I could. You could not imagine our poverty today.

I had to make excuses, like any battered wife. I would blame myself, try to convince his mother, that this was from the war, from the shame of surviving as a kamikaze. At times, when he'd tire of beating me or his mother, Masunori would just collapse in a heap and cry from the searing guilt he felt. "It should have been me," he'd yell out. "I'm a coward. I didn't have the strength to sacrifice myself with my friend. I didn't have the courage to die for my country. I'm so ashamed," he'd scream.

It's easy to judge now, but the harsh toll these times had on everyone, you just cannot judge too harshly. If a person has personal problems, they can seek help in a healthy society. But in a harsh one like post-war Japan, there is little sympathy, and no tolerance. No one wants to hear your problems. Everyone is just trying to survive, and all burdens seem as great as your own. Many people broke.

And he would break down, too, at the end of his tirades, and beg our forgiveness. Despite the beatings, I could never muster any anger. I just felt very sorry for this man, and his mother. She especially seemed shamed by his behavior, because she would apologize to me even after he had beaten her. It was taking an incredible toll on the woman, perhaps more than all the dirt, poor food, dirty water, acrid air, and lack of medicine did on her body. You could tell that she had been raised with class, in some kind of prosperity, before the war. "I never raised him like this," she'd say, over and over, bent over and looking down in the dirt that was her natural view of life.

At night, when I bathed her, all of her sorrows would come to the fore. She was old Japan – a once proud young woman from a good home who had been brought to her final state by years of ill fortune, war, famine, and finally, the living casualty of her shell-shocked son.

"My Masunori wasn't like this as a child," Kishi-san would say to me. "He was such a good boy, but the war changed all that." Kishi-san would then break down in tears.

"Dearest mother-in-law," I would say, "I know it's the war's fault, not Masunori's."

As we spoke and I continued to comb, strands of Kishi-san's hair would come out in the comb. Malnutrition meant that it fell out all too easily. It made me so sad that I would stop and stroke her hair with my hands instead of the comb. I would also wash her back for her, reduced though it was to nothing but skin and bones. Kishi-san would apologize to me, saying what a waste it all was, what a terrible waste.

"Now, Kishi-san, I am Masunori's wife you know." I would tell her, helping her into her newly washed kimono.

Masunori hadn't returned for weeks after the birth of his son, and his mother urged me to go find him. I knew he was traveling with the troupe, and that they were making money, but I was still puzzled about why he had been gone so long. So I set off with Kazunori on my back and headed to Kagoshima so that he could see his son. It was a common site in Japan then—women hunkered down on the roads, carrying their newborns. We really had no other way to find him, since we had no telephones, of course.

After days of making the rounds, I finally discovered them late one night in a small village where the troupe had erected a little lean-to covered with a tatami mat to sleep. It sat behind their stage. The troupe was pulling up stakes in a clearing, but my husband wasn't there. They all seemed visibly shocked to see me, especially with a baby and just pointed toward the lean-to, where they said he was sleeping. It was about 11 p.m.

There was only weak lantern light all about, so I walked carefully toward the darkened lean-to. I assumed he was sleeping, so I quietly flipped up the mat to enter.

I stumbled about, then I heard a woman's gentle voice. After my eyes adjusted to the dark, I saw him lying in the embrace of another woman.

The world seemed to pull out from beneath my feet. My heart immediately knew what had happened, but my mind was still enveloping the scene before me. He jumped up, appeared at first scared, then angry. I thought he was going to start beating me again. He seemed like he was going to run toward me but then hesitated. He seemed to be thinking what he wanted to do—chase me or let me go.

He chose to stand and watch as I ran off into the darkness. I just started running as hard as I could with the child on my back. I ran through the streets until there were no streets, and the last lantern lights grew into wisps. I knew vaguely that I was heading into the mountains, but I just trudged upward on the unpaved road. I passed one village, then another. I was beyond tired and really felt nothing despite the fact that I had been walking all day. I was carried to just a single thought: kill yourself. If I had to explain it, I guess I just wanted to run so deeply into the darkness that my death wouldn't even be felt. I had no idea how I was going to do it: drown in a stream, hang myself with a rope, or slash my throat with whatever sharp rock I could find. I was tired, dirty, and wailing, though I didn't even hear the wailing until others began to talk. When I began to notice my surroundings, I seemed to be in the road of some tiny mountain village. Lanterns flickered on, as villagers awoke, and men began to peak out of their houses. They probably thought I was a ghost or some forest creature, wailing, and walking about their dusty road in the middle of the night. Finally, I heard doors slide open and footsteps on the gravel. A lantern hovered near me and a lone farmer asked me what was wrong.

Then the baby started to cry. I had completely forgotten about him. I took him off my back and we cried together. I can only imagine what this farmer thought, because I don't remember making any sense through my wails. Soon other doors slid open and it seemed like the entire village was out on the street. And everyone was so kind, saying "It's going to be ok, It's alright." Someone called a policeman, and soon I was escorted to his house, the only one with a telephone. Everyone followed us to the house, so it was like some sort of procession. The policeman stumbled about his tiny house, waking his wife and tried to figure out what had happened. He knew immediately that I wasn't from their village, so he asked me if there was anyone I could phone for help.

323—that was the only number I knew. So the policeman picked up the phone and called my father. I heard voices mumbling but I was still beyond making any sense of what was going on. The policeman gave me some tea and rice, and after a short while put me to sleep with my baby on a futon. The first real memory I have of that night is realizing that I had no breast milk for my son. We were both so malnourished.

CHAPTER 16

Back to Yatsushiro

My eldest brother Kazuo, arrived the next day to bring me home. He had recently returned from the war, but he was still waiting for his name to be cleared as a war criminal by the American occupation authorities. He hadn't committed any war crimes, but because he was **a** ranking officer, he was under investigation like all of our leaders. In fact, Kazuo was a hero; a man who had been involved in one of the few undisputed acts of bravery during the war. A meteorologist by training, he had been involved in the 1943 evacuation of thousands of soldiers and civilians from an island called Kiska, in the Aleutian Islands. My brother, being a meteorologist, had helped plot for the escapees, a daring operation which was done under the cover of a heavy fog. This was later depicted in a famous movie, *Taiheyo Kiseki No Sakusen: Kisuka*, starring the legendary actor Toshiro Mifune.

Kazuo was a kind, gentle brother. As *chonan*—the first born—he had an important leadership role in the hierarchical Japanese family structure. And he would live up to it in advising and helping me over the next difficult year. But for now, there was little to be said. It was all very awkward of course. It seemed to take the longest time for the train to Yatsushiro to arrive. I didn't speak much to my brother, a stranger to me for most of my life since he was away at war. I was only concerned about my baby. I was wondering what would happen to his father and me. But I had nowhere to go but home if I wasn't going to kill myself. It wasn't like a defeat, but it was against every instinct I had. I was in shock, though. Not thinking. Just following orders, drifting from place to place like a floating weed. I had decided to live my life on my own, but what had I accomplished. I had followed a poor, troubled man, lived in poverty, and given birth to a son who seemed to have no future. No I was heading back to the very place I had fled. Again, I thought of dying.

But when I saw my baby's face, I couldn't kill myself. And when I saw my brother's face, I felt some responsibility to live, to try to atone for my shame. My brother asked me questions, but I don't remember my answers.

When I arrived at the house, of course I had to crumble and beg the forgiveness of my father. My dad just stood there and finally said, "You must be hungry. Eat." He stared at my face, then he picked up the baby and hugged him.

For the next few months, I lived my life as the village failure. At home, in the streets—everyone knew me as the disgraced daughter—profligate, shameless, abandoned, and burdened with child. I can only imagine what message that may have sent to other daughters who wanted to set off, or fathers who worried about their children learning the craft of the theater. I had confirmed every negative instinct of these parents and underscored the egocentric image of an artist here in this harsh, closed society. Technically, neither my child nor me existed. Minamata city hall and all its records had gone up in flames in an air raid so I was never actually entered into the *koseki* (the family census) under Masunori's family name. My father said to me, "Never you mind. Just you stay here. You can stay here with us forever." Everybody in the family was so kind to me that my brother must have told them that I had intended to kill myself.

I never smiled; I hardly ever talked to anyone. It was very cold at home. My mother treated me as an unwanted houseguest, though she warmed to my son. I had dishonored our family in a way no amount of my dad's bad behavior ever could. It was quite unbelievable to anyone in our social class what I had done. They had heard about such things, read about them in stories of disgrace, but nobody seemed to actually know of any scandalous daughters like me. But looking back, I can forgive it all. People were struggling to build a new society, a new community. It's essential in these times that people stick together. Especially in Japan, where so much is defined by membership in a community, the social order is important. Today, a daughter might not think twice in following my footsteps, but in the 1940s it was very radical and dangerous.

It was several months before my headstrong ways emerged yet again. I decided I had to start standing up for myself so I enrolled at a dressmaking school that was established in one of the local temples. I worked at the fish market during the day, and at night I went to school and learned how to make dresses. This continued for about one and a half years until one day the teacher asked me to help her instruct other students. I gained more confidence as a result of being asked to assist, and I began to think that this trade might be my ticket out of Yatsushiro.

Slowly I emerged out of what could only be described as a profound depression. When I go down, I really plummet to the bottom of the ocean, and it's very difficult for me to come back up to the surface again. But slowly, I seemed to float toward the sunlight and it was the dressmaking that helped me. People began to notice me practicing, experimenting on cloth at home. I was smiling more, and people were smiling in return. I think my father had feared for the longest time that I would try to kill myself and maybe the baby, so he was especially glad to see me responding to something positive. My son was doing very well and getting a lot of love at home. Nobody held me against him and he was raised always knowing that I was his mother, even though in many families a child would be told such a woman was his sister or aunt to lessen the shame. My family never did that to me.

About Masunori, I saw him maybe two or three times again. Once, he came to town and stood waiting for me one day when I was leaving a public bath with Kazunori. I ran home and refused to talk to him. He just followed along, yelling, "Please wait. Please wait." Eventually, we had to meet in front of a magistrate so that I could get legal custody of my son. It was necessary because it would legitimize my son and make his life so much easier in the coming years. He would not be stigmatized as an illegitimate child. I didn't talk to my husband at all during the proceeding which lasted less than an hour and ended with him giving me full custody. "Katsuko, in this way you'll be able to live your life the way you want to," my father said as he inscribed Kazunori's name under his own in the *koseki*, Japan's all important indicator of a person's familial status and social origin. The consequence of this was that Kazunori and I now appear on the register as brother and sister.

Kishi-san, Masunori's mother, died about a year later and I was told that when they prepared her body they found a picture of me inside her robes. I felt much honored by that gesture. It told me that she still loved and respected me, and that I had been a good daughter-in-law.

Masunori died three years later, having abandoned his acting to work in a miso factory in Minamata. He drank himself to death, as so many former soldiers and survivors did in those difficult postwar years. Many people died quickly in those first few years. They were the hidden toll of the war. Thinking back, I can only feel sorry for my first husband. He was once a good man, a good son, but he was a victim of the conflict just as if he had been killed in battle. He could never put aside the fact that he was meant to be a kamikaze for a war that ended too soon.

CHAPTER 17

New Life in Sales

Kazuo, my oldest brother, took a job in the new weather station in Fukuoka. He had been talking to me frequently on the phone, and I think he realized that I too had to leave the village. "I want to work! I want to be someone," I'd tell him. I was desperate for ideas; I needed to make something of myself. He invited me to live with him in Fukuoka, where I could study at a higher level as well as get a job at one of the large department stores that were emerging in the post-war economic boom. He talked to father for me, and they agreed that this might be a good thing if I were allowed to work, go to school, and better myself in Fukuoka. I think they both realized the future for me was bleak in Yatsushiro.

One of the largest department stores—*Iwata-ya*—gave a test to prospective employees. It wasn't much—basically, common sense questions about how to treat a customer, make a sale, and handle cash. But keep in mind, Japan was still a backward nation at the time and there were tens of thousands of poorly educated, desperate people from remote countryside villages flooding into the cities. These were prestigious jobs, really, the best a woman could get then, and they wanted to make sure they were getting bright, energetic women. I passed the test and got a position in the men's wear department, called Maruzen. A lot of dressmakers had shops in the building and during my free time I could stop by, chat, learn things about the newest styles, materials, and techniques that were filtering in from places like New York and Paris.

I felt somehow God was looking down on me and although I had done something stupid and had made a horrible mistake, perhaps I was being given a second chance. I don't know how else to express it, but I was sure that I was on the right path. My brother had a very high-ranking position in the weather service in Fukuoka, and I stayed with him in a very nice apartment. Every morning I'd take the trolley to work, and I was earning a very good income. After three months I saved up enough money to find a room in a nice two-story house very close to my work and study. I don't really know if I deserved it, but I did know that I wasn't going to make any more mistakes. I wanted to be independent, strong, and capable of supporting myself. Everything I did at this point was toward that end. I never felt desperate nor fell into the dark trade like many impressionable, young girls did at that time. I never prostituted myself. But being a young woman in such a country, such an uncertain yet exciting time, was not easy. I'm sure I made plenty of mistakes, but I did what I felt I had to do to secure my lasting freedom. All I know is that when I started putting all my energy into dressmaking, everybody's attitude toward me seemed to change.

I also delved into flower arrangement—a very important traditional craft in Japan—and achieved a fairly high level. I obtained the license to teach it myself and this helped me earn more savings. Dressmaking, flower arrangement, working in a department store—these were the only respectable things a woman could do at night, so I had a great deal of independence and income as a result.

Once you were hired at Iwata-ya, you had to go through six months of training at the department store, learning how to approach a customer, determine his needs, and properly flatter, cajole, and lure him into the final sale. As with all things Japanese, this was a carefully calculated ritual. And I loved it. Salesmanship just came naturally to me. I loved to chatter, flatter, and cajole. I loved to see a man walk in—I was working in the men's department at the time—and instantly I could deduce his needs, likes, and dislikes. I loved guessing how I'd approach someone, sizing them up quickly enough to bolster their ego but not to embarrass them.

The clothing men and women wore were still drab. It mostly consisted of shapeless wartime garments, designed mainly to ward off the creeping cold caused by the lack of fuel for domestic heating. There was a huge black market in clothing, cooking tools, and especially metal pots. Cooking bowls were being stamped out of aircraft aluminum left over from the war. Japanese military leaders scraped off a share for themselves and sold it to the black market, small manufacturers, and retailers. The same with clothing. It was a common site to see men, women, and children wearing parts of old army uniforms, which only debased the idea of militarism further in the postwar mindset.

But slowly, companies began to rehire, the construction industry took off, and extra income began showing up in people's pockets. As you can imagine, people wanted to drink, eat out, find that special someone, and have a good time. And for that, they needed to dress up. I relished picking colors and cuts for these men, who probably were not yet used to having a woman dress them. This was still quite a radical, modern departure for Japan at the time. I had no doubt that many of these men were shy, lonely, perhaps depressed. They needed someone to tell them they looked good, to adjust the cut of their jib, to find the right coat, the right pants, the perfect matching shirt, and tie. You had to be delicate with the fat men and firm with the arrogant types—those who thought they looked good in practically anything. Because I had studied dressmaking, I think I had a leg up on the other sales girls. I had the instinct and training for how cloth fell over a body. I could see where alterations would be necessary, where this spot needed to be tucked in, or that place needs to be loosened up. I quickly let the customer know they were dealing with a tailor not just a sales girl.

It was an art and a science, but I never had to remind myself what I was there for—to make the sale. I remember always thinking, "How would I sell clothes to God?" Because the customer was God—that's what we were taught. Would God ever want a pushy, aggressive harpy selling him a suit, or would he prefer the gentle yet strong ministrations of a friendly young girl?"

After I saved a little money, I got my own apartment—a four-and-a-half tatami mat room—a tiny place but my own. Fukuoka was the largest city on Kyushu and I had all the delights of a working girl in the big city. I really settled in for a while and thought that department store life was perfect for me. I was the number one sales lady and I could see myself moving up the chain of command, even though it was still very much a man's world. I lived in Fukuoka for the next three years and continued to study dressmaking.

CHAPTER 18

Design School

But again, the old urges to do more, to learn more, started to resurface. I realized that I could only learn so much in a regional capital. The latest styles and fashions just took too long to filter in through Tokyo from the rest of the world.

After doing some research, I filled out an application for the Ito Mohei design school in Tokyo. I took the entrance exam and passed it, and then had to take a two-day train to Tokyo for a personal interview. I apparently impressed Ito Mohei, because I soon got word that I had been accepted to his school. My mind was in Tokyo already. The site of this sprawling city, viewed for the first time as I approached it in the train, seemed like the rest of my life was unfolding before me. I had been stymied by the size of Fukuoka, but Tokyo seemed to go on forever. My brother was shocked, and my father was shocked that I had taken such a step. Still, after I explained my goal, my father gave his permission. He didn't know Ito Mohei or his prestige, but he probably realized there was little he could do. It was important to me that I had his blessing. Everyone was shocked that I actually passed this difficult exam. I had a little bit of savings and a friend who I could live with in Tokyo. Because I had done so well at Maruzen, they were interested in helping me find a job with a Tokyo store. I took a job working in men's clothing with *Takashimaya,* the largest department store in Japan. That did impress my father.

Everyone knew Takashima-ya, the Macy's of Tokyo.

I arrived in Tokyo for good in 1950 after two days of travel. I had a strong feeling that I was going to succeed now. Yes, I was a single mother. Yes, I had left my child behind. But this was a common plight in Japan at that time. There were many widows, many broken relationships, many lonely single mothers. I was just one more. If I had stayed in Yatsushiro, my life would have ended soon, I felt. I cannot even imagine what I would have done. I honestly felt like this was the best course for myself. If I was ever going to be a good mother and provide for my child, here was an opportunity that I couldn't let slip by. The bitter truth is that the country's defeat provided me these opportunities by breaking Japanese society wide open. If we had won the war, I would have been forced to marry someone in Yatsushiro. There would have been no escape in such a country, which would have been drunk on its machismo and militarism.

The excitement I felt at setting off for this new school, with elated hopes for a promising future, and the idea of living alone in a big city, was confronted with the reality of postwar Tokyo, a vast labyrinth of rubble, rice rations and reconstruction. The huge devastation of the war was still everywhere. Pre-war Tokyo had literally been a city made of paper. The firebombs that the Americans dropped on the city caused some of the largest slaughters of the war, though they were overshadowed in many minds by the atomic bombs dropped on Hiroshima and Nagasaki. Hundreds of thousands died as their homes went up instantly. Women and children seeking to flee had been cooked alive, as if on a skillet, on the vast steel bridges that crossed the city's rivers.

The result was a landscape of broken stone and mountains of burned wood as far as the eye could see. The reconstruction was well underway when I arrived, but the size of the task was immense. On one block you may find workmen and trucks scurrying back and forth to erect new buildings. On the next, you'd find dirt streets, stores, and bars built out of the rubble. With handmade signs swinging in the breeze, broken windows, and shattered doors; these streets looked like some dusty ghost town in the American western.

The contradiction was borne on faces too. For every newly employed *salariman* or sunny schoolgirl in her crisp uniform, there seemed to be dozens of veterans and their families wearing torn, dirty military surplus clothing. There was no bracing for it. At every corner of the city you might turn down Optimism Avenue or plunge through Desolation Alley. Although much of the massive masonry structures, like the old banks, samurai homes and the Imperial Palace, were still intact, much of the city was drab and worn.

I was lucky because I was living in a fairly middle class area of the city. If there had been any destruction, it had long been repaired by 1950. I rented a room in a nice house—the sister of a friend from Iwata-ya—and spent my days either taking the train to school or to work. I lived in a suburb called Mitaka and spent about 40 minutes every day on a train to school.

I attended school all day on Monday, Wednesday, and Friday; then I worked full time on Tuesdays, Thursdays and the entire weekend. I was always busy. There was no time to rest. At Takashima-ya, I developed a rapport with the clothing suppliers of the men's department and soon moved up the ranks of salespeople. I was always jotting down notes—about colors, cuts, and tie lengths that I thought would help us sell more suits. Every week the owner of the suit company came by, and I made sure I caught his eye and gave him my notes. I was combining what I was picking up at the design school with what I observed among the customers. I pointed out that Japanese were short people, and that suits had to be cut to flatter them. They shouldn't be miniaturized versions of western suits, but coats and pants that didn't need alteration. It was a great time because Japan was hungry for ideas about fashion and was humble, and open to ideas from the outside world. But I was still a woman, and it became very clear to me that what's commonly referred to today as—the glass ceiling—was for a female in Japan, something barely off the floor.

CHAPTER 19

Bar Girl

Even after a year of working, money was still a problem and I needed a second job. Tachikawa Air Base was the nearest American area in Tokyo, so I decided to go there and look for work. The people with disposable income, of course, were the Americans. So if you wanted to make money, you went where the Americans could be found, and worked in their bars, restaurants, and military base stores. Tachikawa was really the heart of nightlife in Tokyo with its restaurants, cabarets, and shops stocked with luxury goods from the United States. I began walking around there at night, looking for a place where you'd find the most Americans, because I figured that would pay the best.

I have to say it was scary, because up to then I hadn't ever talked to an American. I had no idea what to expect, and there was also the fear of being labeled a prostitute, or *pan-pan girl.* The first cabaret I walked into hired me, but they were concerned because I couldn't speak any English. So I bluffed. The job was to get American soldiers to buy drinks. What a woman had to do was just look pretty and act interested in whatever the soldier wanted. I don't drink much alcohol, but if I was serving drinks to soldiers all night, they were going to want me to drink too. I got to know the bartenders well and had them pour me Pink Ladies, a relatively lighter drink that I could drink without alcohol and nobody could tell the difference. I also had them pour it to me in smaller glasses—and make it a deeper pink—so the drinks looked strong and sweet.

In just two days of this work, working three hours a night, I made three times what I made at the department store every week. I drank swiftly and moved from table to table, getting the soldiers to buy more drinks. The Americans spent money like water, and I needed it desperately. I had to pay rent, tuition, and occasionally have my young son brought up to see me. I applied some of the same salesmanship techniques I learned at the department store to the bar—I treated the customers like God. Americans had a very polite manner. They weren't like most Japanese men, who treated serving women like their personal slaves. They were always most interested in whether or not you'd drink with them. I never had any bad experiences. Most were young boys, kind, and gentle who seemed lonely and far from home.

Tokyo was a city far beyond anything I had ever seen. It was much larger than Fukuoka and moved at a frenetic pace for Japan. My first impressions were that there were so many, many people, and that they moved and talked so fast. I first stayed in Mitaka, which was a small neighborhood on the western edge of the city. The school was nearby, and between my two jobs and studying, I slept very little most days. At the time, Ito Mohei was most famous for what we called three-dimensional design. Before him, dressmaking was mainly done with patterns set atop cloth. Though it may seem silly now, Ito Mohei had studied how to make dresses on mannequins, which was quite revolutionary in Japan. Our days at the school was spent sketching out designs for evening dresses, which was also very rare, and then cutting fabric, and designing "live" on the mannequins. We had to learn how fabric fell over the shoulders, hips, and breasts. How it looked in light, and how it moved when one walked. In that sense, it seemed like an extension of my *Nihon Buyo* training in theater.

In the beginning I was very nervous because I was just a girl from the countryside. I was from a very poor family and there were girls at this school who were from some of Tokyo's most elite families. After class each night, many would want to go out to cafes and talk about design. I didn't have the money for such extravagances, so I always had an excuse ready that wouldn't expose my lowly background. I also had to bluff my way through speaking like a city girl. The language is rough in Yatsushiro. It's like a rural southern twang to the ear of a sophisticated city dweller. It was almost another language. I had to learn to mimic the city accent and choose my words carefully at first. The class itself required a level of confidence in style and elegance, from the way the teachers and students carried themselves, to the manner in which the class was taught. Soon I had erased my Kyushu dialect. I did well in class, but being around all of these sophisticated people took its toll. Though I could change my style, I wore a lot of poorly made, inexpensive clothes that couldn't fool anybody. I'd often get depressed, lonely, and wonder if I could ever graduate from this school, much less pay for tuition for the next three years.

CHAPTER 20

My First Property

As I made more and more money drinking Pink Ladies, I decided to move closer to the base. I rented a small single room in a building that had a public bath. I was always looking to make more money, and one day I glanced behind the building and saw a vacant lot. There was maybe 3,000 square feet there, and I thought it would be a great idea to build houses on it. I figured I could build four small, one-room houses on this land. This was one crazy idea, but I had begun calculating how much money I had saved, how much I could borrow, and what it would cost to rent that lot and build the first house. There was clearly a market. Some of the American soldiers, foreign diplomats, and private contractors liked to live off base, and I thought I might be able to rent the houses to them. At the time, Tokyo was a series of buildings and farm fields where just about anything was being grown. There was a lot of construction but nobody seemed to be paying attention to this spot. So I found the farmer who owned the land, a man named Kimura-san who lived in far-off Sunagawa. I told him I wanted to build a house that could be made into four apartments on the land, and that it could be lucrative for us both because I had planned on renting it out to Americans. I assured him that I could come up with the money. I had saved quite a bit for a woman my age. I rarely dined out or enjoyed the night life that Tokyo had to offer with its many shops, boutiques, and everything to entertain. However, my constant companion was always the thought of how I could better myself, and establish a future enterprise that my son and I could live off of. I ultimately accumulated money from various sources; my savings from my day job at Takashimaya, together with my evening job at the hostess bar; a small loan from a local bank, and surprisingly my father had even chipped in. When my father got wind of my scheme from my brother Kazuo, he was astonished that I was doing so well at work, school, and now I was even showing some promise as a business woman.

I continued to plead with Kimura-san, "Please, would you lease that plot of land to me?" I asked him earnestly. He thought I was crazy, a simple country girl. Why would he do such a thing, he asked, lease his land to a stranger? But I just hounded him, going back there every day to talk to him, to see if I could come up with some formula that would entice him. I just wore him down with my persistence, and he saw how serious I was. I think he realized that I was smart enough to pull this off, and that he'd profit from it. There was a carpenter in the neighborhood, so I drew a sketch of the house I wanted and took it to him to build.

What is a house but a different kind of dress? It's just another layer of clothing to protect you from the storm. The house I wanted would have two rooms—a living room and a bedroom. It would have an American style shower and an American toilet. I studied the design of homes, looking at some magazines and books, and sketched out my design just as I would a dress. You had to get approval from your neighbors to get any electrical work or plumbing done, and you had to know how much cement, wood, and tile you'd need. I calculated every cost with the help of the carpenter. I went back to the bank hopeful I could borrow more money as the costs increased, but they took the conservative stance, and said it was too risky. But the carpenter saw I was serious, and he staked me for the balance I needed. My dream was coming together.

The most difficult aspect was buying the lumber. You had to purchase the wood and transport it from the mountains, because that was where you found the best and the cheapest lumber. The carpenter taught me all of these tricks about construction. He saw me working so hard, coming to the lot every day, and checking on the progress of the construction. He couldn't help but help me. Here I recognized my power of persuasion, and used it to bargain everything from the cost of supplies to hiring contractors, always assuring them that they would get something out of the project. Every day I went to the bar, drank a lot of pink ladies, and continued to save money. I never stayed at the same place in the bar. I always moved around, funneling in as many customers as I could with the one thought in mind of completing this project. A key element of being in the service industry, is getting noticed and having people recognize you. I discovered that as long as you smiled, a kind G.I. would always notice you. If people remembered you, the next time you're recruited to serve more drinks. Being popular with the patrons was the one way to make more money for the house, and this also allowed you certain privileges, like choice locations in the bar, and nights when the big spenders would come in. Being a bar girl was the lowest thing a single girl could do at the time, but it was also lucrative and a means of survival.

I worked two years as a bargirl and built the house in six months. Nobody knew about this secret project—the house—and nobody among my classmates knew about my job as a bargirl. Keeping these secrets made me physically ill with fear at times. I didn't want other bargirls to know about my expanding fortune, and I couldn't risk my elite classmates learning of my disreputable income. It would have scandalized the school, though I'm sure other girls were in the same position all over Tokyo at the time. Still, I was always in fear that someone would walk in, someone would see me, and it would get back to the school. I would be expelled. At the bar, I worked under a fake name—Kimiko. The house was another matter, because a woman going into business like this would raise the question of how I got the money. It was frowned upon—strong women taking initiative. As soon as I finished the house I rented it to an American businessman who paid me 10,000 yen, which was quite a sum in those days. You could say that this was my first foray into real estate, and to this day it is one of my greatest successes. I did it from scratch with barely a yen to my name.

CHAPTER 21

My American Husband

It was about this time that I met my first husband—the man I'd marry—Ronnie. He was an American G.I., a sergeant in the U.S. Army Air Force, who hit it off with me, and started coming back more and more to see me at the bar. The bartender spoke very good English, and he would translate for us, but soon we developed our own little codes and phrases to communicate alone. He invited me out on a date, and I took him to see the house. I was so proud of it. He was just shocked—shocked that a little barmaid like me could summon up the will and the money to build her own house. He was also impressed that I was learning dress design. I had a two-room apartment at the time, a tiny place, but one room was given up totally to my tailoring work. I had designs on the wall, a mannequin, and rolls of cloth everywhere for my lessons and experiments.

I was eight years older than Ronnie. He was just a young man of twenty-two, but that never was a factor in our relationship. We became close, and it was through him I began to entertain the idea of moving to America. I can honestly say I hadn't thought of it before, even though it was the goal of many bargirls to lure G.I.s into marriage and leave the country. A woman's prospects, especially a woman with a history like I had, were grim in Japan at that time. Still, in Tokyo, I knew I'd be able to survive and prosper on my own. I was tough, determined, and I had the business sense to make money. So

I never felt that I couldn't survive as an independent woman. But through Ronnie I began to think more and more about the nation. Japan was rebuilding, but I knew it was going to be very tough for the next several decades. America, by contrast, ruled the world. Especially in terms of fashion, design, and business; America was the place to be. That was one big reason why I became closer to Ronnie.

I can't honestly say it was love for me, and that was the way I thought at the time. I'm not sure how he felt. I think he was more impressed with me as a strong young woman than as a pure love interest. I really think he wanted to help me first and foremost. That was the type of guy he was, very charitable. Kind. Not oversexed like many of the G.I.s.

We got married in a chapel in Tachikawa. It was very simple. I just raised my hand and that was it. It was 1956. All I was thinking about in those days was finishing school as quickly as possible and eventually selling my house. I never told my parents that I was getting married. It would be one more of a series of difficult blows, and I had put my father through so much already. In the back of my mind I thought some day I would bring my child to America, but I didn't know how this was going to happen. If I had spent all my time worrying about theoe things, I would never have moved forward. Sometimes you just have to move forward, trust that you will correct your past problems, and concentrate on the future. That's what I had to tell myself to keep going. Otherwise, I would have collapsed in depression like so many women and men did in those difficult times.

In 1958, I finished school and sold my house after which we moved to Ronnie's home in Wisconsin. I cried the day I graduated from the school because it finally seemed that I had achieved something free of scandal or pain. I was now a designer with a degree from a prestigious school. I had sold my house, paid off my loan, and pocketed some 100,000 yen, which was quite a sum of money back then.

I was very nervous about moving to the United States. I didn't know what the country would look like or what to expect from his family. I could imagine that many Americans still hated Japanese. I could not blame them. We had just fought a war and I was still somewhat fearful. From the little I had read or seen of news clips, I guess I expected that all of America was New York City. Little did I know that I was moving to the American Yatsushiro.

What lessened that fear, I believe, was that I was moving to the German Midwest, the place where many second and third German Americans had immigrated over the last fifty years. Many still had distant relatives in Germany. A few still spoke German and I think they had lived through a time of conflicting emotions themselves. If anything they were so nice to me, so welcoming. I encountered very little racism. The town was so small, really just a single downtown main street surrounded by small blocks of residential streets. I believe they didn't know what to make of seeing an Asian in their little town. Because there was a Chinese family also living in the town—there seemed to be one Chinese family in every American town—most people assumed I was Chinese, too. For the next several years, I had to fend off numerous offers of introductions to other Chinese families living in Wisconsin.

We moved in with his family in their small house before we got a place of our own. Then, two weeks later, Ronnie had to report to work at the Pentagon in Washington, D.C. He just left me with his family. His mother was a nurse, and his father ran a small business. The town was dominated by the regional hospital, and that provided jobs for most people. What was most odd to me was that nobody seemed to walk in this town. Even if it were just to go down the street, Americans would get in their car and drive a block or two to the town square or the local department store. I was the only one ever walking, it seemed, which just increased my isolation. I didn't speak very good English, so most of my days in this small town were incredibly boring. There just wasn't anything for me to do, nobody to talk to. I began to explore and see what opportunities I could find. It was novel at first, but after a few months it grew very uncomfortable despite how nice everyone was being.

My parents had no idea what I had done. I wrote them a letter from the United States explaining, everything and it was one of the most painful moments of my life. I couldn't face my father after putting him through so much, so I felt this was the best way. I had always been the black sheep, and I told them this in the letter. Everyone had this bad idea of me anyway. I didn't really dwell on it. I apologized to my father for what I was doing, but said that I would come back some day and get my son. That I always knew. I explained to him how I felt about Ronnie, how I thought I had a better chance to improve myself in the United States, and that I didn't want to bring any more shame onto him. I'd been through so much, I thought, in a very short life. I was twenty-nine, had lived through a war, eloped with a lover, been disgraced as a wife, and abandoned with my child. I had survived, and many had died, that was true. But I wanted to be something special, and I thought I had that inside me. I was not *bonkura.* I felt I owed it to myself to continue moving forward. This was selfish. There was no other way to put it, especially in a culture that prides itself so much in acting for the group, not oneself. But I felt I had to be true to my selfishness, or I was only going to make everyone around me miserable and probably die before my time.

Ronnie sent for me, and I moved to Virginia to live with him. I began working out of our apartment as a seamstress. I had met a tailor in Oshkosh, and had learned some of the American terminology for tailoring. I was picking up the language but I tried some new things to market myself. As I worked on their clothes, I'd provide Japanese food for customers to munch on. I wanted to set myself apart. Ronnie liked to laugh at me—how I did business. But we were growing apart. I saved all my money, and I began talking about moving to New York. There was a student from my old school living in the Bronx. I didn't know her well, but I had a name and a number that I had written. She sent back an invitation to come check out the fashion scene there. Six months later, I flew to the city for a few days and fell in love with it.

Ronnie knew something was up. I think he was slowly realizing that I wasn't going to settle for the life of a military wife in small towns and bases. Again, I knew it wasn't love for me, more like respect. And I think he grew to understand that too. There were never any loud screaming fights between us. The relationship lacked that kind of passion, and besides, he was far too nice a gentleman. Rather, it was a gradual drifting away, as I looked further into what my next step would be. He seemed almost impressed that I was taking this great step. I had the money from my house, and the money I was earning working as a seamstress. So one day I just told him I was moving to New York, and that was that. We stayed married for a year, and we talked often but we never lived together again. This was in 1960.

CHAPTER 22

The Big Apple

I moved into a room in a house where an old friend, a former student at the Ito Mohei School, was now living in the Bronx with her husband. The house was owned by a kind Italian store merchant, who was renting the house to us as a group. I enrolled in a design school, nothing in comparison to Ito Mohei and attended classes there for the next two years. I was mostly bored there, though; the teacher used to ask me to help out in designing dresses, discussing new fashions, etc. I felt very honored, but still I was a little mystified. Ito Mohei's 3-D methods hadn't yet carried over to New York, which I thought was more culturally advanced than Japan. The American style seemed very sloppy, not very detail oriented. It was all very disappointing, and for the next year I felt I was struggling. I was living off a stipend from the U.S. Army, for military wives, but I was still desperate for cash. So I took a job with Stella Brown, a dress shop that specialized in evening wear and worked there as a fitter. For the next two years this was my routine; working all day then going to school at night, but I knew if I was going to stay in the United States, I had to learn English. So I began taking lessons at night at a school for immigrants near Union Square. That was where I met the man who was going to be the next husband.

I saw Ronnie only two more times over the next year. I never had the desire to get back together with him, and we parted sadly, but amicably. We formally divorced in 1963. It was my fault, once again, I had let my selfishness guide me. When I get an idea, or a passion, it guides me at the expense of those around me. I had written one letter to my parents, but I never heard back from them. It was still very difficult for unsophisticated Japanese to write to the United States at this time, and I hadn't given them any instructions on how to reach me.

Katsuko in NYC

Tadao Suzuki and I were the only Japanese in the English class, so naturally we started sitting next to each other. He was the son of an eminent toymaker in Japan, and his father had used his connections to send his son to apprentice in the United States. After a brief stint as a scholarship student at Cornell University, he grew bored and wanted to work in the toy business full time. He was working at a toy wholesaler in Manhattan, overseeing the shipments of the toys coming in from Japan, which were then sold to the city's prominent toy stores. This was the heyday of "Made in Japan" when the country was largely growing on the surge of cheap imports to the United States, and the rest of the world. The wholesaler was a very kind Jewish man, and he and Tadao were very close. He was like a second father in America to my boyfriend.

After a brief courtship, we married in 1965. We had a brief civil ceremony in Manhattan, followed by a small party at the toy factory. I had told him everything, about my first husband, about Ken, about my life with Ronnie. But he acted as if he wasn't very interested about my past. He was only interested in our future, he told me. He didn't tell his family, which was an elite Tokyo family. They certainly would not have approved. Tadao had grown up with a nanny for himself and each of his siblings, he was accustomed to being catered to, until after we were married. He didn't want to deal with their resistance, or what he assumed would be their protests. This was without even knowing my past. If they found out about that, there would have been serious repercussions, maybe even disinheritance. By the time we informed them, it was after the birth of my second son, *Isamu*, in May of 1965. Tadao was a twin, and when his brother learned of our marriage later, he was shocked that his twin would do such a thing. But Tadao was always his own man. He didn't really follow any path. He was always saying it was good that his parents couldn't write English, and mail a letter, so he didn't have to deal with them. He was this headstrong and independent in everything thing he did. It was what I loved about him. Soon after we got married, he quit the toy business and started working for Nippon Express, the Japanese FedEx, located at Kennedy Airport.

Shortly, after giving birth to Isamu, I discovered I was pregnant again. This was a very difficult time. I was working from home, trying to take care of my newborn son and expecting a third, with little or no help from my husband. My third child was a girl, and we named her *Rie.* With each child born, I'd made the effort to reach out to my family, and they usually responded with a loving note and baby clothes for the children. I began communicating with my family more and more and started to inquire about bringing Kazunori to the United States. My husband realized how much I missed my son, felt that it was my duty to raise him, and supported my decision.

CHAPTER 23

Kazunori

Kazunori, or Ken, wrote that he wanted to come to New York, even though I told him it was difficult for me to take him right now. But he kept writing, many letters, saying that he wanted to come to New York. It broke my heart, and finally we decided to bring him over.

Ken came to live with us shortly after we were married, and we enrolled him in an English language school. He was sixteen at the time, and the other children didn't like it at first. I had seemed to come full circle with my father, bringing a child from the past into my household just as he had brought Hideichi to live with us.

We enrolled Ken into Haaren High School on 59th Street and 10th Avenue. At that time, the school was ninety percent immigrants from China, Yugoslavia, and Latin America, so Ken was certainly not isolated as a newcomer to America. Still, it wasn't easy. Not speaking a word of English, he failed miserably for the first six months. But then, something clicked. The language starting coming to him naturally… you'd begin to hear more English even in my conversations with him. After six months he excelled so rapidly in math and science that he graduated as salutatorian of his high school. He then matriculated to City College of New York.

In 1966, he was eighteen years old and the Vietnam War was heating up. Just one year after enrolling in college he received a draft notice for the U.S. Army and was called in to take the physical. It was almost as if he willed it to happen. Somehow, he got it in his head that it was his duty to fight, even though technically he was still a Japanese resident alien. Ken was very fond of his Uncle Kazuo, my eldest brother, who became a legend in Yatsushiro for his service during the war and served as a role model to him.

I think Ken took all of this to heart. He knew there was a draft in the United States, and he was subject to induction in the U.S. Army. He could have gone back to Japan and sat out service. I was especially fearful that if he went to Vietnam, he'd be mistaken for an enemy soldier and shot. He should go back to Japan. He was Japanese, not an American. This is what I wanted, but he insisted that he wanted to fight the war. He wanted to become a soldier, and told me he wasn't going to change his mind. I fought this decision but he kept pushing, invoking some sense of Japanese honor that he had somehow picked up growing up in Yatsushiro.

He passed the physical with flying colors and with his A-1 classification was expected to join the fight against Vietnam. The day he went to the recruitment office, the recruiter for the Navy was fatefully away from his desk at the time. In his place, was a recruiter for the U.S. Marines. The U.S. Marines was a department of the armed forces that only took volunteers and after learning that his enlistment time would only require two years, Ken signed on the dotted line, not realizing that he had just signed on to fight at the forefront of the battle. He was sent to the Marine boot camp at Paris Island, South Carolina, where he did eight weeks of basic training. The training was fearsome and his drill sergeant was a survivor of Iwo Jima. He was obviously marked by that experience and he channeled some of that anger on my Japanese son. Despite being the smallest recruit and the only Japanese soldier he managed to survive and go on to San

Diego where he was trained in guerrilla warfare. The final training took place in Okinawa, Japan where they finally discovered that Ken only held a Japanese passport and still spoke problematical English. Ken was then given a choice of remaining on the island or being sent to Vietnam to fight. Ken chose to fight and was immediately sent to Da Nang, South Vietnam.

The year was 1967 and Ken fought in at least eleven combat battles. On February 5, 1968, he was wounded fighting against the North Vietnamese in the old ancient capital of Hue. Ken being small in stature, was struck head on with an enemy bazooka, resulting in a wound to his head and a gash to his right arm from flying shrapnel. He was immediately sent to the medivac in the Philippines with his bone exposed and nerves destroyed in his right arm. After three months of physical therapy and rehabilitation in Hawaii, he regained full use of his arm. Thereafter, he was sent to Quantico, an officer candidate school in Virginia, for lighter guard duty.

I quit Stella Brown and started working out of my apartment, using kimono fabric to fashion dresses for the Asian community, especially the Chinese and Vietnamese, who had strong, growing enclaves in the city at the time. I felt this was a market that the more established retailers were ignoring, and I thought I could do good business with them. I was right; I did quite a good business out of my apartment for the next few years, at the same time trying to raise my children. I rented a room on the street level of the building where we lived and opened a dress shop called *Kotobuki.*

Ironically, the same year that my son was fighting in Vietnam, I unintentionally became involved in the anti-war movement in the United States through my talents as a dressmaker. A young former model and her husband, Shirley and Michael Hale, driven by a desire to show the Vietnamese as both people and a culture, had began commissioning *ao-dais,* the traditional long, flowing Vietnamese dresses, from me. They were selling them in a shop they had rented near the Village that they were calling a *protique,* a boutique that was pro-Vietnamese culture, though it was also interpreted by some as being a "protest boutique" — Michael made no secret of his anti-war views. This occasionally caused problems because the protique sat a few blocks from Tompkins Square, which at that time was the scene of frequent clashes between anti-war hippies and the police. The store had been attacked on at least several occasions.

One thing led to another, and word about the store apparently made it to the *New York Times*. They wrote an article, dated July 3, 1967, that gave me some good publicity. The Times wrote, "The seamstress who makes the ao-dais here is Mrs. Katsuko Suzuki, who is of Japanese descent. Her son, Kazunori, 19, is serving with the Marine Corps in Da Nang." The article continued on: "Mrs. Suzuki's ao-dais are made of colorful silks, silk blends of brocaded fabrics that the Hales buy during weekend excursions to Orchid Street on the Lower East Side." After that article appeared in the *New York Times*, the number of clients who had heard about me from somewhere or other started to increase.

One hot day in August, I heard a knock on the door of my apartment on Third Avenue and 86th Street. My two little children, Isamu and Rie are crawling around the floor that I had to step over them to answer the knock. Standing at the door, barely recognizable was my son, Ken. He was wearing a marine uniform covered with dirt and looking worse than a homeless man. The day before, I had just received a telegram from the Defense Department informing me that Ken had been wounded. The last person I expected to see at my front door was my son, alive, and smiling. Apparently, he thought it would be a good joke to surprise me and show up out of the blue. My knees buckled and I fell to the floor, holding on to his legs, shaking, and crying in disbelief that my son was home. My children looked at him and wondered who this stranger was standing before them. He was emaciated and hungry. His appetite longed for something other than army food out of a can which I quickly went to prepare. I brought out my usual Japanese dishes of rice, pickles, and *miso* soup. I could tell Ken was in heaven. Eating my simple country dishes put him at peace for the first time in two years that he said, "He could finally feel like the war was over."

CHAPTER 24

Suzu Fashion

This in turn led me to opening my second business, 'Suzu Fashion." Instead of selling garments like a normal store, what I would do was take samples of my designs around to stores and then make garments based on the orders that they placed. My designs were very particular when it came to the kind of fabric used and the standard of the needlework, and a single garment cost in the region of 30,000 yen — $30 or $40, which was quite expensive for a dress in those days. Nevertheless, the orders continued to increase. At the time there were four members of my staff, including myself. However, with me doing both design and needlework, we found ourselves unable to keep up with orders. I devoted myself to the design side of things, expanded the staff and entrusted some with the business side; a mistake that soon would come back to haunt me.

Several months later, one of the staff members left on a routine business trip with twenty or thirty of my designs. I soon discovered that he was marketing those garments to stores around the city. He never came back. My designs were stolen. To make matters worse, he also took with him the linchpin of the business, the client list. Without this list there was no way to continue operating. And I didn't even have the money to sue this guy. I felt like I had been raped. I was consumed with rage for quite some time.

And yet, eventually, I thought to myself, wasn't this perhaps the time to call it quits? The business had just started to tick along nicely, when this happened, but I wondered if perhaps a higher force was trying to tell me something. Even if I was determined to persevere, it would be awful if I went bankrupt. An entrepreneur without an eye for the future of a business can be a real liability to others. When I thought about the children, I realized that I simply couldn't afford to make the sacrifices necessary for the running of a business. I closed the business, however and continued to make dresses from home.

In those days, Tadao worked for Nippon Express USA. He would go out to work in the morning and come back late at night, eat his dinner and then go to bed. On Saturdays he would play golf. That was his whole life. But I was restless once again. I asked him for advice on this matter but was taken aback by his unexpected reply:

"It's not my job so I don't know..."

While I fully came to realize that we were both emotionally detached from the marriage and disconnected from one another, his reply still left me speechless. I was earnest in asking his advice about whether to carry on or quit my business. His advice, however, amounted to, "It's your business. I don't know."

It was so despicable that I seriously considered leaving him then and there. The only thing that stopped me was the thought that separating would not have been good for our children. It seemed that both at home and in business my troubles were just getting deeper and deeper.

As I agonized over what to do, the memory of the pomelo tree that had grown in our garden when I was a child came to mind. My father's friend had sent his company into insolvency and then fled to Taiwan. As a result my father had had his home taken away from him, but he hadn't given it a second thought, I remembered. Even so, I thought, bankruptcy would be a terrible thing. On top of that, the cloth and needlework involved in my business imposed considerable costs. If I were to borrow money and a similar catastrophe were to occur… Surely it was better to get out now while I was still free from debt. I employed several people at the time, so my agonizing continued day after day. I couldn't depend on my husband. It was ever so lonely not having anyone to turn to for advice. I agonized over what to do for nine and a half years before I decided to quit the dressmaking business.

CHAPTER 25

The Corcoran Group

Many years passed. I thought about going into real estate as the market continued to heat up in the mid eighties in New York City. it also seemed perfect for me at this stage of my life. There was little or no overhead except personal energy, I was a natural saleswoman, and I had lived in New York City long enough that I had acquired a great deal of local knowledge. I took the real estate sales license exam and passed. Still, though, I felt disconnected from my husband. I had no real sense of what the future would bring, and at this point I lacked imagination for seeking a new path.

In 1989, when I was well past the landmark age of 60, I lived with my husband and family in Long Island. Due to several previous real estate investments that I had made over the years and once again my idea of renting out rooms to well paying tenants, I was able to sell both of our houses in Queens, NY for a beautiful ranch home in Commack, Long Island. My husband still worked in his white-collar job for Nippon Express. I was a full-time housewife and very restless. Although, we lived in this beautiful house with numerous *bonsais* my husband had planted, my kids were now grown, my husband was busy nurturing his *bonsais*, and I needed to channel my energy elsewhere. My son seemed to sense I was restless. Finally, one day, Isamu, whom we all call Sam, asked, "Hey, mom, why don't you try working at The Corcoran Group?"

He thought that I might make a good real estate agent with The Corcoran Group; a real estate firm, which was founded in 1973 by Barbara Corcoran, and dealt exclusively with high-end properties in the New York area. There are around 2,500 people working for the company now, but in those days, it was still a venture company with only fifty very hard-working employees.

The idea of going for a job interview at the age of sixty did, in all honesty, give me pause for thought. But my son had a contact at the company and helped set up an interview. I set out that morning with the address jotted on a slip of paper. The office was on the eleventh floor of a building at the corner of Madison Avenue in an area that mainly catered to advertising companies. I don't know why I even bothered — I wasn't that enthusiastic about the idea of working there, and I didn't really feel I had the necessary fluency in business English, let alone the terminology of the real estate industry.

I checked my watch, and saw that I still had an hour as I stood in front of the building. I decided to pass the time until the interview by wandering around the area. I came upon a man selling what looked like clothing at the curbside. When I approached to get a better look I saw that it was, in fact, hand woven blankets that he was selling. They were all so elaborately embroidered, so brightly colored, and beautifully patterned that I just froze right there, lost in admiration. One of the blankets in particular took my fancy and I thought, "I must have that!" And so, I handed my money over and took the blanket.

Almost immediately I regretted the impulse buy. I'd forgotten all about my interview. The hand woven blanket was thick and heavy. Carrying it in both arms, I fretted over what I'd just done. Whenever I'm interested in something, I tend to act precipitously. It is, at the same time, both a good and a bad aspect of my character.

As I pondered all this I realized I was going to be late for the interview if I didn't hurry. So, I picked up the bulky blanket and walked back to the building.

As I waited for the elevator doors to close a white woman suddenly slipped in. She glanced at me, looked at which floor I'd pushed, and said, "11th floor? Same here. I'm bigger than you are, so why don't I carry that for you?"

I was so surprised by her next move, when suddenly she took the blanket right out of my arms, and looked as if it was the most natural thing to do. We stood there in silence for a few moments, the door opened and she handed the blanket back to me. "Have a good day!" she said and bounded off down the hall. It happened so fast that I didn't have a chance to even thank her.

The blanket and I headed into the Corcoran Group's reception area. The receptionist had seen the whole encounter, and I assumed the woman was a Corcoran agent, so I asked the receptionist if she could thank the kind lady who had carried my load.

"That lady" she said, "was Barbara Corcoran, the president of the company."

I surely looked shocked. "Really? That woman was Barbara Corcoran?" The receptionist replied that yes, it really was her. I was amazed; I couldn't believe that the president of a company would do something like that.

"That's just Barbara" the receptionist smiled, "she's always helping someone, even if she doesn't know them."

After an encounter like that, you begin to think fate may be intervening, guiding you toward a new chapter in your life. I'm always looking for signs on my journey, no matter how small or how far in the distance they may be. I took heart from the turn of events, and boldly asked if it would be possible to leave my blanket with the receptionist. She was only too happy to oblige.

A few minutes later, one of the office doors opened and an elegant woman appeared. Her name was Esther Kaplan. Everyone smiled at this place, I noticed. Everyone seemed never too busy to greet each other, or extend a small courtesy.

Esther introduced herself and escorted me into her office. Immediately she asked, "Do you speak English?"

What else could I say? As I had sat waiting to be called, I had realized more and more that I wanted this job. It was no longer just a lark. I understood enough English to answer her questions.

"Yes."

"Do you write English?"

"Yes, only a little."

Esther paused. She looked at me sadly.

"This is an American company. How do you expect to get by here if you can't speak and write English?"

It may have sounded rude, but I understood her point. But I wasn't giving in. Something about the encounter with Barbara had emboldened me. Her kind manner, her warm face — these all convinced me that this was a good company to work for, the kind of company that would give someone like me a chance.

I jumped out of my chair and said, "I can do it!"

Judging from the look on Esther's face, I must have shocked her. I shocked myself. I don't know where the words came from, or what drove me to be so bold. But I repeated, "I can do it. Please watch me."

"Okay, okay," she said, eager to calm me down.

But then fear took hold. I realized if we continued talking, she was not only going to get a good grasp on my poor English, but she was going to realize I really knew next to nothing about real estate.

Telling her the story of my little investment property long ago in post-war Tokyo — even if I had managed the vocabulary to do it justice — wasn't going to cut it. It probably would have only convinced her I was delusional. Before long, security would be called to escort me out of the building. All I wanted to do now was run out of the room.

So, I said to Esther, "That's OK?"

She smiled charitably and nodded. "OK."

And that was that. I gathered my coat and purse, picked up my heavy blanket at the counter, and went home. The whole thing had lasted 20 minutes. Lesson learned. I felt a little bit crushed — all I could think about was how much I wanted to work for Corcoran. But I also knew there was not a chance I was going to be hired.

So much for my analysis. The following Friday I was at home doing the usual housework when the phone rang.

"Katsuko?" asked the caller. It was Esther Kaplan, sounding very cheery, "Please be at our office at nine o'clock next Monday."

I'd been hired. I was shocked, and I'm sure I garbled my thanks. In fact, I realized I was just repeating "Thank you very much," over and over, which surely didn't convince her any more that I could speak English.

How, after that interview, had they even considered hiring me? I had been sure that with my wretched command of the native tongue they had realized there was no way I could sell property in Manhattan, of all places. But the next day, as if to convince me it wasn't a dream, a letter arrived in my mailbox confirming that Corcoran had indeed hired me.

On Monday morning I arrived at Corcoran at 9 a.m. sharp. Esther met and escorted me into the inner suite of offices.

"Katsuko, I simply couldn't forget your greeting and your

smiling face," she said. She still tells me that often, recalling our first encounter.

In those days there were only about fifty employees at Corcoran. Looking around the office, I immediately noticed that almost everyone was white. It concerned me, but at the same time I felt oddly comforted. New York in those days was already a multi-cultural city, and I felt that being Asian might give me an edge in sales to the rapidly growing — in size and affluence — Asian community. For some reason, whenever my back's to the wall it causes my heart to pound with excitement.

Every Monday the staff at Corcoran held a lunchtime meeting. It's a great way to get a jump on the week — Mondays always require some jump-starting — and for new employees it's a good opportunity to gauge the atmosphere in the office. Instead of sitting down, I decided to stand in the back of the room, listen, and take a visual measure of my new colleagues. And, quite frankly, I wanted to avoid being publicly questioned. So I stood near an easy exit.

The meeting started immediately on time — a good sign. But then everyone started speaking at once, or so it seemed to me, the poor English speaker. Suddenly, I felt like I was in a crash course at Berlitz. People were speaking so rapidly, across the myriad of the city's many accents, that I had trouble understanding. I just stood there in silence, my eyes darting back and forth, trying to follow everyone. But I understood nothing. If someone had asked me a question, I probably would have panicked and ran from the room. I was tensed to bolt through the door at the first sign someone was turning toward me.

It was pure fear. Could I ever make it at this company? Even if I did like Barbara Corcoran, doing business for her was altogether a higher order. But as the meeting started to wind down, Barbara stood to speak. And what I saw amazed me.

Barbara seemed to speak using her whole body. It was like some kind of exotic dance that I, in my isolated existence, had never really been exposed to. This wasn't body language. This was something else entirely. Her body seemed to move with every word, her limbs and stance flexed with some unique emphasis or gesture that seemed perfectly to make her point. It was an amazing performance, like watching a great politician or military commander. She controlled the room.

All I could think was, "This is for me! I want to be like this woman!" I realized that maybe I could make up for my poor English by teaching myself such body language. Or develop my own body language. It may seem silly, but it was like an epiphany. In Japan, we have great speakers, charismatic, with commanding presences — my father was one such man — but among woman, even former actresses, such open movements are rare. Japan's culture seeks to minimize body movements, gestures, and facial expressions. Its arts, its drama, its religious rituals, stress careful, highly choreographed steps, bows, twists, and turns. Its business culture favors conformity, group thinking, nothing like the strong commanding individualism I saw in Barbara.

One of my hallmarks is that I'm quick to adopt what impresses me. Using Barbara-like body language I would be able to make myself better understood to English speaking customers. I could also project confidence to my future clients. I felt hope welling up inside me and my resolve to work at Corcoran grew.

CHAPTER 26

Sales Strategy

Four days later, that Friday, I was sitting at my desk when Barbara called me over. I entered her executive suite nervous and a bit frightened at what she could possibly want from me already. Then the body language began.

"Katsuko, what can I do for you?" she asked, staring straight at me.

I didn't have time to think, so I just blurted out: "Advertising."

"What do you mean, Katsuko?"

"I want to advertise on TV," I explained, "but it costs money to advertise on TV so it's difficult for me to do it by myself." I explained some ideas I had about reaching the Japanese immigrant community in New York, how I might better target them if I could focus on their local Japanese language newspapers and newsletters.

The conversation lasted for about five minutes, and Barbara didn't say much. She just listened. I went back to my desk, and five minutes later she walked over.

"Katsuko, here are your advertising expenses." she said, placing something on my desk. It took me a minute to focus at what I was looking at. It was a document signed by Barbara Corcoran and a $10,000 voucher. I had to catch my breath. I had never seen so much money in one place, not to mention in reach. At the time ten thousand dollars was worth about ten million yen. Tears came into my eyes and I struggled not to weep right there like a fool. I realized that, Barbara, this woman I had only bumped into carrying a blanket like a bag lady two weeks ago, was putting a huge amount of trust in me. I was happy, but at the same time I realized accepting her trust in me was a huge burden. I had contributed nothing to her company, yet her she was, handing me a pile of cash and more importantly, trusting that I would not waste it. If anything, my ambition and zeal to do right by her was so strong I thought I'd explode. It was all I could do to think carefully and strategically and not run out onto the street to buy advertising willy-nilly.

And so, I sat there calmly for a while and formulated my plans.

Advertising for me with that amount of money meant a TV commercial. And if I was going to advertise on TV, it would be with a Japanese TV station. At the time the only Japanese television station with a branch in New York was Fuji Television. In those days there was one American newscaster who was famous among Japanese viewers: he was known among them as "Fuji Television's Michael."

He had a one hour program every morning from seven till eight. He was a gaijin but his Japanese was fluent — he nearly spoke as well as a native. If I was going to make a splash in the Japanese community, then this was my best shot. I picked up a phone and made an appointment to meet him at his New York studio in New York.

"And what kind of commercial were you thinking of?"

I laid out my vision. The TV screen was to be filled with the name "Katsuko Suzuki" followed by the catchphrase, "Providing you with high-end real estate properties." At the end of the commercial my phone number would appear on the screen in large numerals. That was the message that I wanted to convey in my commercial. I added that I didn't mind if the name of the Corcoran Group also appeared in small lettering on the screen.

Michael just chuckled. "You are a funny one, aren't you, Mrs. Suzuki?"

I wanted to spread the name Katsuko Suzuki — the brand Katsuko Suzuki – to as many Japanese living in New York as I possibly could. I bought one fifteen second spot for a week for $3,000.

Next I set my sights on print, especially a publication called the OCS News. It no longer exists, but at the time it was the best in the New York City for news about Japan. I placed an advertisement in the magazine that carried the same three point message: "Katsuko Suzuki. Providing you with high-end real estate properties" followed by my contact details. That ad costs $250 every time it ran but I used it for the next 18 years.

Finally, I set my sights on the TV Japan channel, a station that broadcast news and light entertainment programs from Japan to audiences in America. Specifically, I wanted a spot next to a program with a strong general audience, something that would offer a cross-section of young and old, male and female. That was the *K haku Utagassen*, or Red and White Song Contest. Think of this as a Japanese "American Idol." On New Year's Eve — one of the most important holidays in Japan — the tradition is for the major network, NHK, to broadcast this hours-long extravaganza featuring the best bands and singers competing in a male vs. female song contest. Making the cut and getting on the show is one of the highest honors in Japanese pop music, and it's viewed in whole or in part by virtually the entire population.

Unlike in Japan, the Red and White contest has commercial breaks when it is broadcasted in the United States. I was sure that an advertisement during this program would be seen by most of the Japanese living in New York at the time. In the age before the Internet, this show especially tied them to their homeland during a very important holiday.

I made an appointment with Mr. Yoshida, the man in charge of the broadcast. When I asked what sort of clients normally bought the available advertising slots, his answer was, "Mostly big companies like Toyota and Honda." Individuals never bought advertising time during the available slots, he told me. The reason was very simple: it was too expensive. But without even bothering to ask the price I pressed on, saying that I wanted to advertise.

Mr. Yoshida was quite obviously shocked. "You want to place your own ad?" he asked.

"Of course," I replied with a smile.

Even after haggling over the price, the cost of placing the ad was still very high. Yoshida-san appeared quite taken back by my zeal, but I hid my growing fear over finding more money to pay for this ad. Seeing the look of worry on Mr. Yoshida's face I said, "Okay, I'll pay you tomorrow. Please bring me the invoice." The fact that it was company money that I was spending no doubt served to lend me an air of self-importance, but it wouldn't mean a thing if I didn't make good use of the money that Barbara had provided.

To Mr. Yoshida's look of surprise I added, "You see, the Corcoran Group don't do things by halves…"

The ad that I placed during the Red and White Song Contest was the same simple combination of name, number, and catchphrase. According to Mr. Yoshida it was unprecedented in that advertising slot. In the past the ads had all been lavish affairs but mine was just printed type with nothing wasted for music, actors, or other production costs.

I continued to advertise in the same slot for a further three years. It goes without saying that it is something that I could never have done alone. In those days I wasn't the only Japanese national working in the New York real estate market but no one else was going about it in such a showy manner.

But it worked. I started getting calls as soon as the ad ran. The money ran out, but Barbara liked my strategy so much that soon after another $10,000 appeared in my account.

A year passed like this before Barbara or anybody else noticed one small problem: I had not sold a single property. Finally, one day I was called into Barbara's office.

"Katsuko, why is it that, despite all of the inquiries that you've had from customers, you haven't tried to sell anything yet?" Barbara asked.

"I don't want to sell, that's why." I said.

Ok, at this point you might worry that I'm insane, and that you've wasted a lot of time reading my memoir before reaching this devastating twist. But let me explain. In 1988, New York was in the midst of one of its periodic real estate bubbles. Even more worrisome, the Japanese were at the peak of their own bubble that would eventually wipe out hundreds of billions of dollars in wealth. The result was that Japanese buyers, flush with unsustainable wealth, were flooding into New York's already saturated market, driving prices higher and higher. Many of them had neither the experience or, really, the wealth to be buying property in a foreign market, especially one as cutthroat as New York's. Sound familiar? There were lots of customers to be had. And yet I didn't try and sell any properties at all. For a broker in the real estate business it was an unthinkable attitude to adopt.

But many of my callers had simply assumed big debts in order to do so. I could tell by their accents, vocabulary and overconfidence that they were going to be nothing but trouble. A non-Japanese would not have been able to sense any of them. My advice to them was, "You should hold back from buying just now." And to those who insisted that they still wanted to buy, I was firm in saying no, they mustn't.

It was a novel concept — a real estate broker who didn't sell property and, even worse, actually shooed customers away. At Corcoran, if you don't sell properties, you don't receive any commission. I wasn't selling any properties and I hadn't earned a dime. Even worse, I was actually costing Barbara money by draining her advertising budget for foreign language ads no one else at the company could fully understand.

My philosophy wasn't a secret. I had earlier told a manager, "Even if it means that I have to go without eating, I am not going to sell now."

At home, it was even worse. I was away most of the time, ignoring the children and not bringing in any money. I had to cut the daily household costs in order to make ends meet. My husband's salary was enough to keep food on the table, but nevertheless, my stance was putting our children through considerable hardship.

So it was just a question of time before I was called in by the president. And so it was that, before very long, Barbara heard about my declaration and I was called into her office. Barbara's face, which was normally so bright and cheery when she spoke to me, was, on that occasion, quite different.

I told her that I didn't want to sell. That was followed by a very uncomfortable, prolonged silence.

"I don't understand. Katsuko, you aren't earning anything at the moment, right? Why aren't you trying to sell anything?"

"Because it would be wrong to earn money like that."

"Wrong? What would be wrong?"

So in my best English, I carefully laid out my reasoning. If it had been money that my Japanese callers had been saving up over time, then I wouldn't mind selling to them. But these were simple people using their homes as collateral and had shouldered considerable debt in order to make their purchases. I knew that there were other Japanese brokers in the market who hadn't thoroughly researched their backgrounds or finances and didn't really care if they could afford the purchase or not. To them, it was only about the commission. But — and I know this sounds very silly, indeed incredible — my conscience wouldn't allow me to sell to customers burdened with debt. And I didn't want to be one of those brokers who didn't care about her customers. More silence. Barbara didn't say anything, and I left the office.

Another six months passed and I still had not sold a single property at Corcoran. I took a lot of abuse and ridicule at work. I'm sure I was looked upon as some kind of token hire, or someone just kept around for charity or even humor. At times I overheard several of the managers talking about me. "Katsuko is not even trying to sell," they would say, "We should fire her."

Americans rarely hide what they think, preferring instead to speak their mind. Even when they knew that I was there, they would still talk like that. It has to be remembered, however, that, at that time, a lot of other staff members were being laid off. Barbara Corcoran is an excellent manager, and one who was quick to get rid of unnecessary staff. In fact, Corcoran had gained itself a reputation in real estate for being ruthless in firing people who didn't meet their standards. It was all true, and I was well aware that some Japanese staff had already lost their jobs. Barbara Corcoran is a woman of great integrity but her decisions regarding personnel are swift. She judges a person based on their personal strengths and professional results.

But Japan's asset price bubble was at its height. I noticed that some callers now were even offering their life insurance as extra collateral. Seeing people go to such lengths in order to come to New York and buy a house made me seriously question whether they were in their right minds or not. It was becoming a fad in New York City for Japanese women to marry an American, get a green card, and then obtain a real estate license and start selling properties.

One day just such a broker asked me the following question: "Where is Central Park?" I thought she must be joking so I asked her to repeat her question. Without doing anything like the proper research into the New York market, this woman had been selling properties to client after client. On top of that, many of these Japanese brokers were busy buying up properties themselves. The banks in Japan, too, were eager for people to buy land and properties in New York. I just couldn't understand the thinking behind it all.

And then, of course, the bubble burst. Those who had taken out loans to finance their purchases found themselves up to their ears in debt. Those who had used their homes as collateral had them repossessed, and a great many people were left at a complete loss for what to do.

When I think about it, the fault of the Japanese was their failure to do their homework. They had fallen into the trap of thinking that, as long they handed over their cash, they could leave everything to someone else. I got the impression that, even during the bubble, customers from Hong Kong had never failed to do their homework about the real estate market. The Japanese, on the other hand, brought nothing with them but their checkbooks. It is for that reason that they met with such misfortune.

Many of the managers at Corcoran seethed at my refusal to sell and told Barbara directly, "Katsuko isn't selling anything, you have to fire her."

But Barbara always said no. "I absolutely will not fire her."

Perhaps she thought that she'd invested so much money in me that she simply couldn't fire me. Other members of the staff, though, weren't aware of the money that she had invested in me. For my part, I could do nothing but express my gratitude to Barbara for making it so clear that she wouldn't fire me. During the period in which I didn't sell anything, I learned a lot from Barbara. She also gave me a lot of ideas.

I speak Japanese with the strong, local dialect of Yatsushiro in Kumamoto — think of someone from Mississippi or Arkansas and you get the idea. The Japanese who were coming to New York to buy properties on the other hand all spoke the formal-style language beautifully. They were largely products of a post-war education system that had standardized the Japanese language. But I think that the fact that I spoke with this accent actually meant that what I said to them had a greater more genuine impact than it would have had otherwise.

On one occasion I received a request from a Japanese lady to show her some properties. She stipulated that the property must have two bedrooms. The property in the condominium that I showed her was on the market for the considerable sum of $1.5 million. The moment she saw it, she wanted to buy it. But I held her back. She looked surprised and asked me, "Suzuki-san, why on earth shouldn't I buy this property?"

"You mustn't acquire all that debt just to buy a house." I explained, telling her to go back to Japan with her savings. In that case, the client headed my advice.

My strategy all along had been that when prices fell back to earth, the clients who I had saved from potential losses would come back to me. They would remember me. After all, how many brokers do you run across who advise you not to buy at all? Soon, I started getting calls from these people. And so it was that I then started to sell properties.

It wasn't just the reputation of the Japanese brokers that suffered but that of New York itself. Investors did an about-face and started saying things like, "I bought a property in New York and I was cheated. All I have to show for it now is a pile of debt."

New York brokers were the targets of their anger. I was among the few — perhaps the only one speaking Japanese — who had saved people money. Among the people who listened to my advice to hold back from buying are some who, along with their families, still remain loyal and steady clients. I felt entirely vindicated for my conviction not to sell. My relationships with my clients are long ones, nurtured over three decades. It's not unusual for them to last ten years or more. I never chase clients that leave me; I simply wish them all the best for the future.

Even when I wasn't selling properties, I was building up relationships of trust with future clients. The condominium properties that I was showing to Japanese buyers were now clearly bargains. And these clients introduced me to new clients, with the recommendation that I could be trusted to do the right thing. A virtuous circle had been created.

Clients who I had prevented from making purchases during the bubble said to me, "Oh, Katsuko-san, you never deceived us, did you?" and then inquired about properties on my list.

Whenever I sell an apartment to a customer there is something that I tell them all, "I'll take care of the housekeeping, don't you worry."

Employing a maid to clean the windows or around the house can cost fifty or a hundred dollars a day. But if I go round with my broom, it doesn't cost a thing. Brokers don't normally go to the extent of cleaning a client's property for them, but it is something that serves to strengthen the relationship of trust that a broker shares with her client.

I like to stress the following point with clients who live in Japan while renting out properties in New York: "Living abroad as you do, you can't possibly know all that's going on with your property. Please leave the responsibility for the cleaning up to me."

So far I've yet to come across a client who has said no to my proposal.

Whenever there is a problem with a property my clients call me. If the water pressure is bad, for example, or the toilet is blocked, whatever it might be, I will go to the property and have a look at the problem. If a repair is required, I'll call a good repairman and get it fixed right away. Usually, these things can be taken care of for about $300. This is fundamental, and not something that should be stinted on. It is something that I always include when drawing up a contract with the client. I want this relationship to last, after all. Aside from giving me a good feeling, and easing their fears, I am laying the groundwork for future sales.

Another reason that I put this much effort into the management of a property is that, the moment you start to cut corners, even a little, the value of the property drops. Many of my clients don't live in New York, and it is quite common for some of them not to visit their properties for as many as ten years at a time. Very often they are unaware of the condition that the property is in. So, if the paint on the outside walls starts peeling I'll tell them, "You have to paint the walls, you know." And sometimes I'll say, quite forcefully, "If you don't paint those walls, you won't be able to rent this property out any more." Several clients of mine who have trusted me to manage their apartments, have saved themselves the price of a maid and have been so pleased with the situation, that they have stayed at the same property for more than five years.

With my dustpan in hand, I'm a scrupulous cleaner. If there's a window high up in the ceiling then I'll get a maid in to help, but apart from that I do all of the cleaning myself. The idea of a broker doing her own janitorial work never fails to make people laugh. But quite frankly, I think the image of me with a mop and broom in hand communicates to the client that they are dealing with a different type of broker. Call it old school, but I think it works. My goal is simple: make the landlord and tenant happy, and give them the comfort to know their property is being looked after.

I once made the mistake of taking the subway home having forgotten to take off my apron. Everybody was staring at me and making quite a fuss. When I looked down I saw that the cause of it all was that I was still wearing my apron. In my apron I look just like a Japanese mother of yesteryear. Walking around the office with a cleaning rag hanging at my waist is an everyday occurrence for me. New members of the staff at Corcoran who are not used to the sight often ask me, "Katsuko, what are you doing walking around with that rag hanging from your waist?"

Many people worry that managing properties in this way must be very hard work for me but, I've never once considered it a hardship. It's probably because I don't share the same ideas about what constitutes hardship as most people. My son Sam will joke with me, "C'mon Mom, isn't it time you stopped working? Your eighty years old! It's embarrassing to have you going around with a dustpan at your age." But I work on the premise that I don't want my clients to spend one dime more than they absolutely have to.

I enjoy selling property to the Japanese. I find that many Japanese understand the value of history and therefore tend to take good care of historical buildings. Having said that, there are certain Japanese individuals to whom I don't want to sell.

Take for example the Japanese who may show up in my office one day with a large sum of money that they must unload on a property. If they haven't borrowed the money, it's been inherited after what is usually a prolonged, very vicious process of quarrelling with their siblings. You can tell these people right away, and I always refuse to work with them. I just know it's going to be trouble. They are dismissive and brusque. With their newfound wealth, they like to lord over you. This was much more common in the 1980s – when it seemed like Japan would conquer the world – but it still happens enough that I'm always on the lookout for these people. New York City is the greatest city on earth – owning a trophy property in it communicates to other Japanese that you have arrived.

You can always see them coming. First, they cannot shut up. They brag about it. One day a Japanese woman approached me with just such a large sum of money and asked rudely, "How many properties can I buy with this much money?" After listening to her long-winded bragging for a while, I finally had had enough.

"I bet you quarreled with your siblings to get that money, didn't you? And I bet you quarreled to such an extent that you'll never be able to make things up, am I right? You'll never be close again, will you?"

To my astonishment, she regarded me with a chill look and replied, "That's right. I wanted the money."

My point, as I tried to explain to her, is that nothing in this life is more important than your family. But she simply couldn't grasp what I was trying to tell her. To top it all, it seems that as a result of the squabble over money, one of her siblings had fallen ill. Regardless, the woman still thought that the money was more important and disregarded my advice entirely. I looked into her eyes and I was astonished to see just how cold the eyes of avarice could be.

For some reason though, she invited me out to dinner. I refused both the dinner and the work that she was offering me saying, "There are about twenty thousand brokers in Manhattan. Any one of them would be happy to help you."

But then she said, "Katsuko-san, why won't you work with me?"

"I cherish the relationship I have with my relatives," I replied, "and everyday I offer thanks to my ancestors. For me family unity is more important than money. My children respect me, and arguing over money is disgraceful. As a result I am the happiest woman in the world. You may have wealth, but that is something that you have shamefully gained by fighting over money. You'll never be on speaking terms again, will you? That's why I can never be your broker."

Overcome with emotion, I started to cry. The woman was looking directly at me throughout, but at no point did her expression suggest that she had understood a single word I had said. My point was entirely lost on her.

Finally, the woman said, "Since you're obviously not interested, please be so good as to introduce me to somebody else."

Naturally, I politely refused her request. I did not want my name attached to hers in any way.

CHAPTER 27

Clients and Friends

My role is simple on its face. I buy, sell, and manage real estate for clients. When I close a deal, Corcoran takes a six percent share of the value of that sale. Properties, upon which the broker negotiates directly with the owner, are particularly good. But a broker really shows the depth of what it takes to be a top broker by building relationships with clients. About 15 years ago I sold a property in a condominium to a Japanese lady for $180,000. The property was a duplex with a flight of stairs leading directly from the downstairs to the bedroom. The ceiling was 17-feet high, which gave the property a really spacious feel. The monthly rent for the apartment after sale was $3,500. The owner lived in Tokyo, and in those days it was often impossible for me to inform her immediately of a change of tenant. For that reason, I carried out most of the property management on her behalf. Situated between Fifth and Sixth Avenue, the quality of the site and its location were excellent. The estimated value of the property rose year after year.

About two years ago I informed her, "You know, this property is already worth more than a million dollars." She was amazed by the news, but before she knew it, the price had risen again, this time to $1.5 million. "Now do you want to sell it?" I asked. Far away in Japan and unaware of the real estate market in New York, the owner was astonished by what I had to tell her. But there is a time to sell and a time to hold. As a property ages one must consider not only the accruing monthly maintenance costs, but the future expense for renovations and upkeep for such property. Unlike Japan, people in New York City rarely hold on to the same property for the whole of their lives. What they normally do is wait for the right moment to sell and then, with the money earned from that sale, buy a new property. This is why I put so much effort into showing clients properties with high added value, which look like they are going to rise in value. The thinking behind this is that it will reduce the risk of the client taking a loss on the deal. I once told Sam, "When you build a new building you absolutely must not follow what all the other builders are doing." At the time I said it, there was a boom in condominium construction, but I explained that over half of the buildings going up would be failures.

"In that case, mom, what should I do?" he asked.

My suggestion was that he build loft-style apartments with high ceilings. The location of his next venture was in the financial district around Wall Street. Many people living in the area, even if they were married and had children, lived there alone. They didn't do this out of choice, but because of the landlords and the types of structures there at the time. Only rarely would a landlord consent to rent these smaller apartments to a prospective tenant if the tenant had children. As a result, many of these executives bought a house in the surrounding suburbs for the wife and children, and they would travel back and forth from their pied-a-terres by train on weekends. If the property was of the loft or duplex type then, even if the children were to play around or run wild, the noise wouldn't carry to adjacent apartments. The landlord could rent the property to tenants with children without concern. When I explained this to Sam, he quickly put the idea into action. Apparently, the properties that he built based on my suggestions are now very popular with people working on Wall Street.

One property I once dealt with was a four-story townhouse that Frank Sinatra has once used as a private club. To me, the name Frank Sinatra didn't mean much. What attracted me was the fact that the house was over a hundred years old, and it had much inherent, historical value. The tiling on the exterior walls dated from the time of the house's original construction. The interior fittings and soundproofing of the house were also superb.

I'd known the owner of the house for a number of years but it was some time before she was prepared to sell. Eventually, though, the owner decided to part with it and I put the property on the market for her. There was, of course, a reason for why she took so long to decide to sell. Just like Japan, there are very few people in New York who are interested in the history of a building itself. Even if the building is famous, it makes no difference to them and often they will tear it down and build a new one in its stead. I wanted to avoid that happening, and the owner was of the same mind as me.

Before I put the house on the market, I asked Sam what he thought about the property. He replied, "It doesn't matter if it was Frank Sinatra's house, it doesn't matter if the building has a hundred years of history, a property development company will knock it down and build a new one in its place."

There were many people from overseas who expressed an interest in seeing the property. That's the power of the Internet. From conversations that I had with them, it appeared that they had heard that there were plans to build a subway station nearby. And indeed, several days later it was officially announced that a subway station was to be built right next to the property. Another thing occurred to me. If the property came with air rights then it would be possible to leave the current building as it was and build a new building above it. After asking Sam to look into it, we found out that the building did in fact come with air rights. The owner was delighted to learn that the building would remain untouched.

Katsuko at age 70, receiving an award from Barbara Corcoran

Carol, the owner, is an only daughter. In the space of two years she had lost her mother, her aunt and her grandmother. She now calls me mommy. Carol had always liked my *miso* soup and one time when she said that she would like to taste my homemade miso soup,

I invited her to my house. When she turned up she was wearing a lovely cocktail dress, so to fit the occasion I served her in the manner of a waitress at a high-class restaurant. I think we have a wonderful relationship of trust.

At Corcoran, each month, the employee who makes the most sales receives an award. The employee who sells the most properties receives a ribbon and the person who sells more than ten properties in one month is awarded a red ribbon. Eventually the time came when I was the person to receive that award. In 1997 when I'd been at the company for over ten years, I sold the most properties in one month.

On that occasion Barbara said, "I just knew that I was right about you! I was so overjoyed that I broke down crying, without a care for who saw me. I was seventy years old.

CHAPTER 28

Getting My Broker's License

One of the most important experiences in my life was the challenge of getting my broker's license. There are two types of real estate licenses: the salesperson's license and broker's license. The salesperson's license allows someone to be employed by a broker and to buy and sell property for which they receive a commission. This was the license I held. The broker's license allows someone to employ salespeople and to start their own company. I decided that I wanted to challenge myself and gain this license. It would be more interesting to run one's own company.

Acquiring the license turned out to be a lengthy case of trial and error, and one which–in the end– took me ten years to pass. When I think back on it, it really was a long, hard road. The examination required a broad range of knowledge from the fundamentals of the real estate business through to legal issues. About five hundred people take the exam each time that it is held, and of that, only a small percentage passed. As I remember, the proportion of women who pass the exam is higher than that of men. I was probably the oldest person to take the exam. I was actively involved in the buying and selling of property so I thought that my experience of the clerical side of the job would mean that the exam couldn't be too hard.

But I seriously underestimated the exam and my arrogance turned out to be my downfall. That first exam ended in miserable failure. But I picked myself up and tried again. I remained very positive. However, when it actually came down to it I never got around to studying at all. I even forgot about the exam for a while and before I knew it, it was time to take it again. I failed the exam again and again, until I found that I was no longer bothering to set aside the time needed to concentrate on my studies. Naturally, I wasn't going to pass the exam in this way, and I found that now, even when I did study I didn't actually learn anything. A vicious circle had been created.

Almost before I knew it, eight years had passed since I first took the exam. I was in a bookstore one day and flicking through the pages of the weekly magazine, *Sh kan Shinch* , when I noticed an article by the movie star *Rentar Mikuni*. In it he was talking about his life as an actor. "When I receive a script for a movie," he said, "I read it a hundred times, no matter what the movie. I find that if I read it as thoroughly as that then I am able learn the role off by heart."

When I read his words, I thought to myself, "That's it!"

Learn it by heart…I felt these words cut deep into my laziness, motivating me to start studying. It might sound naive to say so, but these words changed me. The feeling I had upon reading them was akin to the feeling I'd experienced when I'd first seen Barbara Corcoran's body language.

I immediately went home and dusted off the massive study guide for the broker's license that had laid neglected on a shelf for so long. I opened the book and got the shock of my life. The pages were crammed with text that seemed to move before my eyes, as if the letters were hundreds of worms trying to crawl out of a bucket. I slammed the book shut. I was already dizzy and I hadn't read a single word. How was I going to do this? This book was written for lawyers!

I seemed to lose any ability I had to read English just looking at it. What did I think I was doing? Who did I think I was, trying something so ridiculously hard? But I stuck to my plan. At times, I literally fell asleep in the middle of the afternoon trying to tread this tome. But each day I vowed that I was going to read at least one page a hundred times. Day after day, it was as if I was studying the Bible or some medieval work of philosophy, I sat hunched over that book like a monk, reading each page over and over again. The tenacity with which I apply myself to things that I like, or which I have decided absolutely must be done, has the power to surprise even me.

Finally, the moment came when I felt that what I was studying had sunk in. So I headed back to the examination center.

And yet, I failed again. I took the exam several more times, but still didn't pass.

By this time, I was on a first name basis with the chief examiner at the testing center. I had become a part of testing center lore.

"Again?" he joked each time I showed up at the center. There surely was an office pool on how many more times I'd take it before finally throwing in the towel. I can't imagine anybody had actually bet that I would pass. But I laughed along with them. I wasn't in any way embarrassed by any of this. On the contrary, I held my head up high and went in with a bit of a swagger. I admit that, in this regard, I am a bit peculiar. Normally, if someone were asked, "Are you here again?" they would feel ashamed and hide their face in embarrassment. But I was quite cheery. Whenever the examiner asked me, "Again?" I would proclaim proudly, "Yes, me again!"

But I failed again and again. Even the managers at Corcoran asked me, "Katsuko, haven't you passed yet? Why do you need to take the broker's exam?" Behind these questions I'm sure they wrote me off as an eccentric old lady. Why struggle, they might have reasoned. I didn't need the license anyway. Some would just shake their head but then ask boldly, "Katsuko, do you really like taking exams that much?"

All I could answer: Because I can. I could take the test over and over again. There are worse ways to spend your time, and I was learning. By this time I'd become a real study fiend. My 'honorable husband' is a very studious type. The ideal vacation for him would be sitting on a desert island with a load of books and a pipe in his mouth. I was becoming like that. At times, it can be like having a teacher around the house. He wasn't any help with my continuous practice for the exams, though, and he was quite disagreeable about the whole thing saying, "Are you still at it? Why don't you just stop already?"

In a very real sense I had come full circle to my childhood as that dumb girl who couldn't seem to pass her exams. But I'd prove them wrong. It's what drives me.

"No," I told him quite succinctly, "I will not stop." And so with conversations like that a regular occurrence, I continued my daily studies.

Or more precisely: my annual studies. Eventually, ten years had passed. I still hadn't passed the exam. One beautiful day, I vowed that this would be the last time.

"If I don't pass today," I thought as I headed for the examination center, "I'll give up my dream of obtaining a broker's license."

I greeted the examiner, took my seat and the exam started. The time ticked down and a buzzer announced the end of the exam. As per usual after the exam, they started to read out the names of the successful candidates. Several candidates burst into tears of joy when their names were read out. My name, however, wasn't among them.

With shoulders slumped in despondency I left the examination center. It was lunchtime so I decided to have lunch in the Japanese restaurant that was located in the lower level of the same building as the center. As I ate my lunch, I decided to give up and go home. When I finished my *udon* noodles, I thought to myself, "Ok now, time to go home." When I looked at my watch, however, I realized that there was still some time until the afternoon session of the exam. On the days of the exam there was always a morning and an afternoon session. So here I went again. I would take the exam one final time. Or so I told myself. It only cost $15 to take the exam, so that was all that I had to lose. And with that I headed back up to the examination center.

The afternoon session started immediately. I stared at the examination paper with shock. The questions were almost exactly the same as those of the morning session that I had just taken! With unbelievable ease, I worked my way through the questions. When the buzzer went I felt that I'd done better than ever before. I stood at the back of the room waiting for the results to be read out. As I waited my old friend the examiner approached me, a large smile creasing his face from ear to ear. "Katsuko Suzuki," he said, "Congratulations!"

Overcome with the emotion of the moment I threw my arms around the man, saying, "Thank you," over and over again. I was absolutely delighted. When I told my daughter, Rie, she cried with joy at the news.

CHAPTER 29

Today

Mornings are refreshing.

I am eighty-two years old now and the secret to my good health probably lies in the way that I spend my mornings. Mornings are the time of day when I feel at my best. They are just right for studying, reading, and writing too. Limited as the time may be, I find that I can really make good use of my mornings.

I typically wake up at six a.m. I used to wake up at four a.m., but I have only grown a bit slower. I have been good at getting up since I was young and I have never used an alarm clock. I believe that is the small town girl inside me still waking up to wait for the fish to come in, or to bicycle off to find my father at one of the many homes of his mistresses.

When I wake up I like to thank my body by giving myself a big bear hug while still in bed. I then say, "Thank you" to my body. I really love these words and always say thank you repeatedly, over and over. I have never suffered from any serious illnesses, certainly not depression, and I am eternally grateful to my parents for the fit and robust body with which I was born.

After getting out of bed, I prepare my breakfast. After eating, before I do my exercises, I pray at the family *butsudan* (Buddhist altar). I believe that this altar has its own karma. When I lived in Queens with my husband and children, I rented out a house to a

Japanese company. The president of the company died in an airplane accident and the contract was terminated. When I came to clear out the house I found this altar that had been very dear to the president. I remembered how he had boasted to me that it had been custom made. Since the employees of the company were all young, none of them were interested in the altar. I ended up taking home the altar, and trying to find a place for this bulky new guest in our small home. It has become a daily custom for me to pray at the altar now.

I have much to pray for. I have been blessed with good children and a constant husband who have stayed with me through various wars and personal tragedies. Against the odds, I traveled from a small rural village in a nation at war with the United States to America's most prestigious city, and I have prospered there.

As for my children, my daughter Rie, or Dia as she is known to her friends, lives in Dallas, Texas with her husband, Jim, and three children. She also worked for The Corcoran Group as my personal assistant for five years before she moved to Texas.

In 1984, when I was working as a dressmaker and also dabbling in buying and renting homes in our vicinity, a friend of mine suggested that my daughter enter the Miss New York Nikkei contest. Using my skills as a dressmaker, I made several gowns for her to wear and to our great surprise, she won the title. Dia was asked during the interview portion who was the person she most admired and she replied, "My mother." Although, I had not revealed the details about my childhood and difficult life in Japan, somehow she knew that I had struggled and made it to America under very precarious circumstances. I wiped my eyes, as tears rolled down my face, and looked up at the platform where she stood. I realized then that my daughter had grown up, and unfortunately I had done very little to guide her to maturity.

I am happy to say that she has turned out very well. She continued her college education in Japan for two years at Sophia University and then came back to the states where she graduated from New York University and met her wonderful husband Jim. I once again used my dressmaking skills to make Dia's wedding dress and perhaps I will one day make my grand-daughter a special dress.

Sam lives in New York City with his wife Sandra Endo, who is a CNN political correspondent. Sam has been in the real estate business for over twenty years like me therefore we share many similarities. He is a special son and his name in Japanese means "courageous". He was born on May 5, 1965, which is Boys Day in Japan and a national holiday.

Sam's birth was accompanied by many complications. At the time I was 38 years old, underweight, and had very low blood pressure. I sensed that something was wrong when I started to bleed early on and eventually I went to see a specialist on Park Avenue. The doctor examined me and strongly suggested that I should abort the baby or risk loosing my own life. I said never. I was not going to give up my baby. Miraculously I managed to carry Sam to eight months, until one day, I experienced a piercing pain. In desperation, I tried to reach my husband but he refused to take my calls, and I was told he could not be bothered while he was in a meeting. I hobbled down the sixth story walk-up, carrying my own suitcase, and hailed a cab to the nearest hospital. The kind taxi driver helped me inside the emergency room where I was prepped for delivery. My main concern at the time was that my baby would be born deformed or crippled. After giving birth, I anxiously kept asking the nurse whether my son had two arms and two legs, repeating my questions frantically, until they finally brought him to me. I immediately noticed a large mole over his right eyebrow and began to cry. He had such a healthy, robust cry, and a full crown of black hair. The nurses tried to assure me that he was perfectly fine and normal. I should have known from his first cries that he would turn out to be strong, brave, and courageous like his name.

Katsuko at age 80, with children, Dia, Sam & Ken

I am sure that the Takenaga blood runs thick through to my children. Sam in particular is very business savvy and has always had an entrepreneurial gift even at a young age. When Sam was fourteen years old he started his own business out of his tiny bedroom. He was making a good allowance by placing emblems onto lighters for a Japanese company. He worked from the moment he got home from school, through the weekends, and even enlisted friends to help him out and make a few bucks for themselves. He was always good at saving money that by the time he was eighteen years old, he invested his savings in his first piece of real estate. This would be the beginning of a twenty-five year career in real estate which he still operates, however, today his purchases are much larger and grander than his first studio apartment.

Ken also lives in New York now. He commutes back and forth to Japan and other parts of the world for his business in the tourism industry. Strangely enough, Ken also has a deeply rooted devotion to Yatsushiro and although, he has not lived there since he was a teenager, he returns often these days to Kyushu, as the Kumamoto representative of tourism and promotional agent for the government.

My husband Tadao now lives in Tokyo. Although we are not living together, we are contently still married and find the distance makes our relationship quite compatible. He enjoys his solitude and the convenience of retirement in Japan where his medical expenses are covered by his Japanese citizenship. I usually visit him once a year, wearing my apron and carrying my zookin. I know he secretly likes that his apartment is cleaned once a year.

I have visited Yatsushiro many times already over the years. I have much to be proud of and I return to my hometown with a sense of atonement and a desire to give back. This was the place where my father taught me to be generous and to look after my neighbors and friends. I no longer feel ashamed and fear the whispers of the old timers. Perhaps I have returned to prove to the villagers that I am not a *bonkura* and I have made a name for myself back in America, or is it the need to make up for my parents' hurt and embarrassment that I had left behind years ago.

An American said to me, "Suzuki-san, you've realized the American Dream, haven't you?"

"No, no, no!" I replied forcefully. I then asked him why he had said such a thing.

"Well, you've made a lot of money," he replied, "that's why."

This reminded me of something that Barbara had once said to me, "Katsuko, if you can make it in New York, you can make it anywhere!"

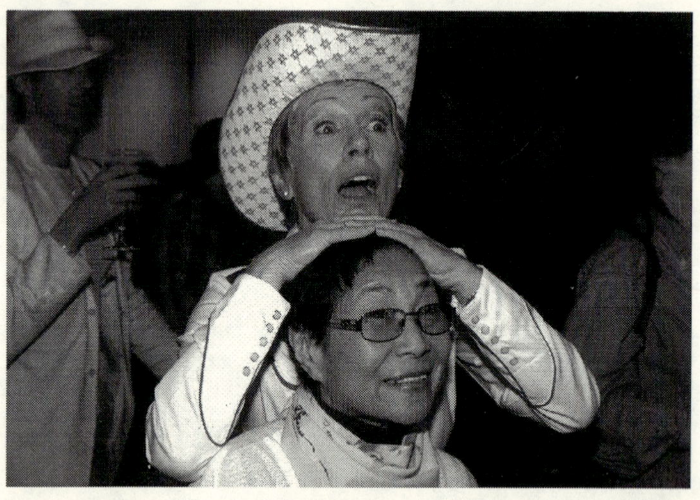

When I asked her why, she explained that making it in New York was proof that you were a success. Success = Money. But I hate this equation. I don't believe that success and money are the same thing. I feel that the New York real estate market is certainly more demanding than that of Tokyo, and clearing all of the market's qualification hurdles is a truly Herculean task. However, I still haven't reached my full potential. I am on my way but I'm not there yet. I have many years to go before I turn one hundred, and to star in that movie that I've promised to my old friends back in Yatsushiro.